8 COLORED PSYCHOTYPES

Behavioral Psychology in Color: Personal Growth and Relationship Building for Every Individual

MICHAEL BORODIANSKY

At the beginning of the last century Sigmund Freud posited that a person's character is somehow related to the sensitive orifices (mouth, nose, eyes, ears and others) on their body.

Back then he did not yet know or was not ready to openly declare that the sensitivity of our orifices governs every area of our lives: from our health to our sexual preferences to the profession we choose to how we conduct business.

This book will teach you about how the kind of person you are depends on your primary sensitive area, as well as how that information can help you throughout your life.

The author leans on gripping and often entertaining stories to discuss psychological tools you can apply to build strong relationships with your children, parents, close friends, and even strangers in business and your personal life.

Michael Borodiansky is a psychotherapist, a business trainer, the author of the psychological vector system, the author of many publications on the art of management and communication, and the father of four children.

Since 1994 he has held 800 training seminars in the USA, Europe and Israel for more than 26,000 people.

This book is published in 6 languages and has long been a bestseller in some countries.

Copyright © Michael Borodiansky, 2012, 2024

9th edition

Translator: Jared Firth

Site: www.psy8.net

Email: mb@psy8.pro

TABLE OF CONTENTS

CHAPTER 2. DEFINING AND ACCEPTING VECTORS

CHAPTER 3. THE RED VECTOR — URETHRA

CHAPTER 4. THE BLACK VECTOR — NAVEL... 108

CHAPTER 5. THE ORANGE VECTOR — SKIN ...137

CHAPTER 6. THE YELLOW VECTOR — MOUTH.. 168

CHAPTER 7. THE GREEN VECTOR — EYES 188

Author's Preface to the New Edition (2024)

Dear reader,

You are holding an extraordinary book in your hands. This is a simple and accessible guide to the mysteries of the human soul, answering two important questions: "How to understand?" and "What to do?" Despite the clear structure of the chapters, you can start reading this book from any point. After all, on every page, you will find something interesting about yourself or someone close to you.

I intentionally wrote it as a lively conversation: as if you and I are sitting in a small circle of friends, and I enthusiastically share the knowledge that once transformed my life.

Yes, it's such a clichéd and sentimental phrase, "transformed my life"... But for some reason, it is the one that most often appears in the reviews I receive from readers from different corners of the world. And now, you too are on the threshold of astonishing discoveries about the connections between your body, character, and interactions with people.

I even envy you a little: I remember the excitement in my eyes when I first saw and accepted my true self — with all its advantages and "flaws," when I learned to read people's characters — from the first moments of interaction, when I realized how easy it is to build harmonious relationships when you know more about those around you than they know about themselves.

The first edition of this book was published in 2012. Then I started receiving offers from publishers in different countries who had discovered the existence of this book and eagerly took up its translation. This led to books in Estonian and Bulgarian. Currently, a Spanish edition is being prepared, followed by a translation into one of the Asian languages.

I want to note that this book will not end for you on the last page. Knowing how often readers crave more details on important topics, I have included numerous references to a wealth of free materials: my articles, short videos, a vector gallery, a vector test, and more.

Well, go ahead, open the book to any page and embark on your journey! I wish you enjoyment in reading and ease in communicating with people.

Michael Borodiansky
January, 2024

FROM THE AUTHOR

Dedicated to Viktor Tolkachev

In 1994 I happened across an unusual seminar. I wouldn't say pure curiosity drew me; instead, it was more a longing for something new. That was a rough period in my life, during which I had neither the personal nor sexual relationships I dreamt of, I earned much less than I wanted to, and it turned out I was not doing anything close to that for which God had given me Life.

The person running the seminar was an energetic gentleman by the name of Viktor Tolkachev, and he promised to teach everyone there over the course of 12 lessons: how to understand themselves and those around them; how to live in harmony with themselves and others; how to achieve career success; and how to unlock all the happiness life has to offer. When he went on to add sexual harmony and a happy family life to that list, the "normal" person I was stood up and headed for the exit. I could tell it was all nonsense.

Once I got to the door, I turned. The speaker looked at me and said without a drop of emotion, "Stay till the third lesson."

Why did I stay? I just wanted to have the satisfaction of walking up to him later and saying, "So? Why the heck did I just waste three evenings?"

I really did head over to talk with Tolkachev a week later, though our conversation went somewhat differently: I told him I wanted to run similar seminars.

"You could make that happen," ViktOr (he preferred it that way, with the emphasis on the last syllable) answered after pondering a minute. Two weeks later he gave me his first book, "The Luxury of System Thought," with this inscription:

"To Michael,

In hopes that you will return the favor"

It was perfectly clear to me what he meant, and I had already given thought to the book you are holding in your hands.

Twenty-one years have passed since then. I feel fulfilled in my profession as well as in my person life. The understanding Viktor Tolkachev gave me of myself way back when has continued to broaden, and it assists me every day as I push forward toward my potential: I publish a psychology magazine, create large-scale internet projects, run training seminars, am building a successful company, and make money doing what I enjoy.

My wife and I deeply understand each other, something that has allowed us to keep that spark alive even after all these years and overcome all of the difficulties family life inevitably throws in your path. Accepting our three kids' natural character traits helps us give them the support and create the environment they need to grow up independent, responsible, and happy. Not only that, but I feel healthier and stronger than I did 25 years ago.

That is why I am driven to pass on my knowledge and experience: over the years I have run over 580 seminars in different countries that have been attended by more than 18,000 people. They now implement what they have learned at work and in their private lives, with some of them even running their own seminars focused on the vector system.

The relationship I had with Viktor Tolkachev had its ups and downs: we argued, tried to prove each other wrong, and each pressed forward in our separate pursuits. Sometimes we disagreed so strongly that we would go for months without saying a word to each other. Once all that was behind us, however, Viktor gave me a collection of articles to which he had contributed. This was not long before his death, and his inscription to this day gives me the strength I need to continue what we started:

"To Michael,

The official successor and favorite

of one of the authors"

Michael Borodiansky
May, 2012

NOTE. Some of the ideas and examples in this book were taken from seminars given by Viktor Tolkachev, while others are from the personal experience of the author and his colleagues. All coincidence with or analogies to Viktor Tolkachev's work should be correctly understood as such.

FROM THE PUBLISHER OF THE FIRST EDITION: ON THE VECTOR SYSTEM

In 1908 Sigmund Freud published "Character and Anal Erotism," an article that made him the source of psychoanalytical study into different character types. After a short description of the psychological peculiarities of people with highly sensitive anuses, Freud had an assignment for those who would come after him:

"We ought in general to consider whether other character complexes, too, do not exhibit a connection with the excitations of particular erogenous zones."

That challenge would not lie unanswered for long. Soon new articles on the subject appeared: "Anal-Erotic Character Traits" by Ernest Jones; "Anal Erotism and Love of Fear and Stubbornness" by Hans von Hallingberg; as well as Isidor Issak Sadger's "Urethral Erotism" and "Erotism of the Skin and Muscular System," both articles focused on other erogenous zones (bodily orifices). So it was that at the beginning of the last century the different character types were briefly described as linked to different bodily orifices: anal, urethral, dermal, and muscular (navel).

The end of the 20th century saw Viktor Tolkachev (1940 — 2011) inspired by the work of Freud and his colleagues to lay out the character types linked to the orifices of the head (eyes, ears, nose, and mouth). As Tolkachev himself claimed, that step was only made possible by his teacher, an academic named Vladimir Ganzen (1909 — 1996), whose book, "System Descriptions in

Psychology," laid the foundation for a systematized view of sensitive orifices.

Viktor Tolkachev in so doing built an entire system that included eight character types, introducing the concept of "vectors" and naming his theory "Applied System-Vector Psychoanalysis." Vectors were understood to entail all the psychological and physiological qualities (character, habits, health, and more) that are linked to one or another of a person's bodily orifices.

In contrast to the accustomed "personality type" (of which there is usually just one), a person can have multiple vectors, each of which has a separate potential from 0% to 100%. Viktor Tolkachev ran seminars on that system, teaching more than 6,000 people over 30 years across Europe and the US.

Michael Borodiansky, one of Viktor Tolkachev's first students, took the vector theory and turned it to practice, calling it the "Psychological Vector System." His biggest contribution was vector acceptance, a new concept that turned out to be key for the practical application of this field.

Acceptance is an attitude toward how one's own vector or that of others manifests itself where we assign it no positive or negative value, do not consider it bad or good, and avoid making a judgement as to whether or not we need it. Acceptance is also acknowledging that vectors serve a purpose, even if we do not yet know what that purpose is. Michael Borodiansky set up a formula for how to calculate vectors and co-authored a test that evaluates natural vector potential and acceptance levels. Anyone who would like to take the Tolkachev-Borodiansky test is more than welcome to at www.psy8.net.

Michael Borodiansky's work is accompanied by other students of Viktor Tolkachev, all of whom are developing the vector theory in a number of different areas, running training seminars, and writing books and articles. Among them are: Ludmila Perelshtein (author of "Careful: Children! Or a Resource for Parents Capable of Surprise"); Yuri Burlan (the System Vector Psychology portal); Alexander and Tatiana Prel (authors of "Why Did We Grow Up Like This?"); and others.

"8 colored psychotypes" brings together knowledge and experience accumulated over several decades. It offers a detailed description of each of the eight character types as well as an algorithm for accepting and realizing vectors in ourselves and others, all of which is built on many practical examples and ready to be implemented in widely varying situations.

Learning about the different vectors and how to accept them will help readers build balanced relationships with themselves and the people around them, feel complete, find their path in life, and follow that path with harmony and happiness.

I hope you are fascinated by what you are about to read and wish you the best as you seek to learn more about yourself.

Anatoly Sekerin

CHAPTER 1. THE BROWN VECTOR — ANUS

HOW IT ALL BEGAN

The Psychological Vector System traces its roots back to a small article written by Sigmund Freud in 1908. Freud used the piece, entitled "Character and Anal Erotism," to describe a type of person who demonstrates a set combination of three character traits (we will get to them shortly).

As children, those people experience problems that in one way or another relate back to a physiological function as well as the organ in charge of it.

Freud makes the claim that this ***particular character type is organically connected to a concrete organ in our body.***

What can we make of that?

When it comes down to it, Freud is claiming that a person's character is built not on their upbringing, the world around them, or any other factor, but on the functions of particular organs. Back at the beginning of the 20th century, that was quite the leap.

It is very well known that many scientists (Hippocrates, for instance) from long ago linked character to the workings of the heart, liver, and other internal organs. Freud, however, took his studies in a completely different direction, driving from the fact that our bodies are closed systems interacting (communicating) with the environment around us via multiple orifices. Those orifices are quite easy to count by looking at where our practically complete skin covering is interrupted:

1. Mouth

2. Nose

3. Ears

4. Eyes

5. Anus

6. Urethra/vagina

7. Skin (to be more precise, the skin's natural orifices: pores as well as oil and sweat glands)

8. Navel* (we can leave an asterisk here, as this orifice closes after birth; regardless, our character is already in place for the most part at that point)

So Freud's main idea was that these orifices, or rather the sensitivity of these zones, profoundly impacts our character. With that said, a century ago he did not yet know (or was not ready to openly declare) that the sensitivity of our orifices governs every area of our lives: from our health to our sexual preferences to the profession we choose to how we conduct business.

Freud goes on to write:

"The people I am about to describe are noteworthy for a regular combination of the following three characteristics. They are especially orderly, parsimonious, and obstinate.

"'Orderly' covers the notion of bodily cleanliness, as well as of conscientiousness in carrying out small duties and trustworthiness."

Do you know anyone like that? If you can think of a relative or friend who is orderly, frugal, or obstinate, you already have a good picture of what this chapter will be about. You may even know entire nationalities that are legendary for their orderliness and frugality.

Freud continues:

"As infants, they seem to have belonged to the class who refuse to empty their bowels when they are put on the pot because they derive a subsidiary pleasure from defaecating..."

Many might pause here, wondering what nonsense Freud could have been cooking up — after all, what do defecation and pleasure have to do with each other? And how could that possibly relate to how people act, especially in business? Well, let us take a look.

Certainly, people are born with genetically defined physical characteristics and builds, particular health concerns, and much more. Our genetics also give each of our "erogenous zones" — those eight orifices in our skin — varying levels of sensitivity. Some of us are born with especially sensitive ears and a sharp sense of hearing, others with especially sensitive eyes and great vision, and so on. With that said, "sensitivity" is much more than simply the ability to take in the world around us; it is a special tenderness or vulnerability exhibited by those particular sensory organs or in a certain bodily zone. In other words, it is a sensitivity to damage, bacteria, and other external influences, meaning that a sensitive eye is both particularly sharp-sighted and delicate in a way that makes even a little speck of dust a major inconvenience. One more characteristic of "sensitive" organs or zones is that they demand their own kind of pleasure: to put it very simply, sensitive eyes love looking at beautiful things, sensitive ears hearing beautiful sounds, and sensitive noses smelling pleasant aromas (of course, preferences vary widely). Sensitive organs maintain harmony and balance (health, in other words) by experiencing an abundance of their particular pleasures. On the other hand, a lack of those pleasures leads to health problems that can be both physical and psychological.

Let's wrap up.

Sensitive zones:

— ...are areas on our bodies linked to one of our eight orifices (orifice types)

— ...enjoy a heightened sensitivity to their surrounding environment

— ...are sensitive to a degree determined genetically

— ...are also sensitive to damage (they are more delicate and vulnerable)

— ...need their particular kind of pleasure (stimulation) and suffer without it

Given that the anal orifice is one of the eight on our bodies, some of us (quite a few of us, in fact) are genetically — from the moment of conception — predisposed to heightened sensitivity in that area. These are the people who enjoy taking their time sitting in the bathroom and other ways of stimulating their buttocks.

Freud grouped people who share that proclivity into the anal character type. Notwithstanding that precedent, the phrase "character type" is limiting, and so we use the word "vector" for our system instead. That is because, first, a single person can have multiple vectors, while a type is just that (there can only be one per person). Second, each vector has a magnitude from 0% to 100%. Our character is therefore a combination of eight vectors (corresponding to the number of our orifices).

People with highly sensitive anal zones in this book are referred to as exhibiting the brown vector, or, for short, *brown-vectored people*. Viktor Tolkachev, on the other hand, called this the "anal vector."

You can take the Vector Test on my site www.psy8.net

FIRST HABITS

So where does what we associate with the brown vector come from?

Let's look at a short story by way of illustration. Imagine a little boy whose mother sits him down on his potty. His anal zone is especially sensitive and has been since birth, and so he particularly enjoys anything that stimulates it. Instead of getting right down to business like his mom wants, he just sits there having a great time. After all, he would happily while away an hour or two if he were allowed — now is just not that time. His mom is in a hurry to get to work, and so she tries to rush her stubborn son along: "Are you almost done? Come on, let's go!"

In one of those fleeting moments where life is at its best, the little boy is robbed of his enjoyment and pushed to finish the job: "Let's go!" What does that do to him? He will spend his childhood and adult life avoiding everyone who is in a hurry or trying to rush him. After all, the longer and more peacefully he is allowed to do what he enjoys, the better he feels. Notice that tranquility and a slow tempo are crucial qualities for the brown vector at any age. With that in mind, stay away from pushing brown-vectored people if you do not want to hurt them (chapter two will cover how best to get people like this moving a bit faster). Continually poking and prodding brown-vectored children sometimes leads to the development of a stutter, neurotic behavior, or even serious bowel disorders. The same applies to adults.

But that is not the end of the story: the mom (the same one who was late for work) decides not to wait any longer, grabs her son from off the potty, quickly dresses him, and rushes out of the house. The boy, robbed of the enjoyment he could have received in the bathroom, at that moment finally does what his mother waiting so long for... And what happens next? His mom most likely takes him back home, changes his clothes, and lightly smacks him on the rear end so he does not do the same thing the next day. However, the loving mother's punishment happens to stimulate the exact area where her son is especially sensitive. Do you think the boy will do anything different the next day? Of course not! He just enjoyed a two-for-one special, which is where brown-vectored children can sometimes learn their stubbornness: they subconsciously instigate situations in which their significant zone is stimulated.

Certainly, there are brown-vectored people who have never once had anything like that happen to them. One way or another, however, brown-vectored children finagle these types of situations such that stubbornness plays right into their hands.

We could wrap up our story with the little boy by letting events play out somewhat differently. One weekend the mom is not in a hurry to go anywhere: "Go ahead, sit there as long as you want!" Finally, an hour or two later the boy happily and finally finishes the job. Children always want to share their happiness with someone, and usually that someone is their mom, so our little boy takes his "happiness" to his mom and delightedly shrieks, "Mom, look what I brought you!" And what does he hear in response? The best case scenario would be something like, "Ew, throw it away!!!"

The little boy cannot understand how something that made him so happy could be gross to his mother, the person nearest and dearest to him. He is so confused that he might even start to develop a deep-seated fear: "There's something wrong with me. If my mom can't even understand me, I'd better keep my mouth shut about what makes me happy. I should probably just be quiet altogether so I never look stupid." As a result, the boy could potentially turn inward, becoming quiet and shut off from the world around him. The brown vector is naturally introverted and phlegmatic, but the degree to which that occurs depends in large measure on childhood experiences.

As you can see, genetic predispositions are not the absolute end of the story. They simply represent a potential that looks different for different people. The other side of the coin, however, is that if a certain potential is *absent* at birth, there is no way it can be developed later.

NATURAL WISDOM

Some brown-vectored people love spending a lot of time

sitting on the toilet even into their adult years, which is why they try to make that area as cozy and comfortable as possible. They install book shelves, hang paintings, and sometimes even set up a TV or phone, to say nothing of all the different lighting and sound options there are to choose from. A quick glance at a bathroom that obviously enjoys particular attention is enough to tell which vector is predominant in its owner. If your friend starts building his home by focusing on the bathroom, you can surmise that the entire building will be clean, orderly, and everything else that comes with the brown vector.

Needless to say, such people pay an inordinate amount of attention to the quality of their toilet paper: it has to be multi-ply and very soft. A brown-vectored person would never dream of using newspaper, as they care too much about their sensitive zone for that.

This kind of soft spot for the bathroom is generally criticized in our society (especially in childhood by parents, teachers, and others), which is why with time such feelings are relegated to the subconscious and the same level of attention is no longer given to the sensitive zone. However, genetically high sensitivity cannot simply disappear, even when we are no longer aware of it. Our Organism still experiences a deep longing for the enjoyment it no longer receives: for the brown vector, stimulation of or pressure on the anal zone.

So what can an Organism like that "dream up" so its significant zone is stimulated? Quite a bit, in fact: take constipation, which includes strong pressure on sensitive receptors. Waiting a few days for the stimulation the end result brings with it is not even a problem, given that brown-vectored people enjoy the anticipation. And how does an Organism make that happen? Simple: digestion is managed subconsciously by our brains, making it understandable why most diseases involving the digestive tract are psychosomatic. For our subconscious, brewing up a little constipation — even lasting a few years — is a walk in the park. Unsurprisingly, many people suffering from chronic constipation are shining examples of the brown vector.

The subconscious is no less creative when it comes to selecting how it will recover: getting an enema not only takes care of the brown-vectored person's problem, it provides even more stimulation for their sensitive zone. You may be aware of some people who regularly have multiple enemas done for "deeper cleansing" and even write books on the subject. Without casting aspersions on such treatments, I would like to emphasize that only those with a pronounced brown vector employ them. Not coincidentally, they are also the ones those treatments help the most.

People without this vector would never try having an enema, and many non-brown-vectored authors put together recovery plans (including for constipation) that include running, fasting, dieting, and much more without ever discussing enemas. They just represent other vectors.

Of course, there are many ways besides direct stimulation of the sensitive zone (using enemas and more) to experience pleasure. For example, anything that involves sitting in one place would be enjoyable for brown-vectored people.

A brown-vectored man might tell a friend, "I'm going to retire, buy myself a rocking chair, and just sit there for a week." His friend asks, "But what then?" "Then," the brown-vectored man happily sighs, "I'll start rocking!"

Rocking in a chair or lilting back and forth in a rocking chair is a frequent giveaway for people like this, while they also love sitting on their hands or with their legs curled under them. If you see a person sitting on their own hand, you can be pretty sure they are brown-vectored.

This kind of person is particularly drawn to quiet, assiduous professions that require long periods of sitting, including writing, accounting, archiving, museum curating, trucking, programming, and law.

Besides quietly sitting in one spot, brown-vectored people enjoy everything that actively exercises their buttocks: biking, crew[1], and of course horseback riding are some particular favorites. With that said, do not confuse a love of horseback riding with a love of horses. While brown-vectored people have no problem dropping the horse off after a nice ride and heading right home, there are other people (black-vectored ones, to be precise) who spend an enormous amount of time with the animals, taking care of them and enjoying the experience of communicating with them.

CROSSING THE FINISH LINE

The most important quality common to all brown-vectored people is their drive to complete everything they do. No matter

---

[1] Brown-vectored people enjoy crew because of the special four-wheeled benches that slide along rails.

what they start, they are never happy until they finish it; getting any satisfaction out of their work requires meeting this deep-seated need.

At first glance, this is a positive character trait that makes brown-vectored people reliable and the best option for important, painstaking work. The downside of that, however, is that they will think up any excuse to stick with the original plan even if a changing situation necessitates a new direction.

Just imagine a factory director responsible for a large team of employees. Market factors change sharply after beginning a new project, meaning that it is time to try something different. While everyone else working at the factory understands that, the director stands his ground: the project will be continued through to its conclusion. There is nothing wrong with his brown-vector intellect; the problem lies with how difficult it is for him to overcome his internal need to finish what he started. That subconscious craving is so strong that stepping away from something that no longer enjoys the bright future it once promised takes a deep understanding of one's self and incredible willpower.

That same tendency holds true in personal life: even a brown-vectored person who understands the fact that they have spent many years in an unfulfilling relationship will still not decide to cut ties. Their partners often successfully exploit that peculiarity for their own purposes.

This character trait can have tragic consequences for the sexual lives of brown-vectored people: something called a "sweet French death." An older man is doing his best to satisfy an insatiable partner, but, understanding that what he can do on his own is not enough, falls back on his habit of finishing everything he starts, draws on some kind of external energy (from the cosmos, perhaps), satisfies the woman, and dies...

Sometimes unscrupulous managers also exploit this quality, assigning one task and coming back with another just an hour later. While they may say the first can be put off in favor of the second, they are well aware that their brown-vectored employees will stay at work all night if they have to in order to satisfy their internal urge to finish both tasks.

PERFECTIONISM AND PEDANTRY

Another crucial quality for the brown vector is *perfectionism*. Perfectionists never see any detail as unimportant, always being prepared to devote a significant amount of time and energy to every last one of them. To be perfectly honest, our daily life would benefit from having more of the people around us take this approach to their work, especially in the service industry. If a mechanic has ever brushed aside a concern by telling you that the car will still drive just as fast as ever, you can be pretty sure they have an under-developed brown vector.

So is perfectionism a positive quality? Sure, though not always. Of course, working with someone who pays close attention to detail is great, though that same attitude finds a dark side when time and energy start running short. For example, a factory director could spend all his time harping on the insignificant defects that are unavoidable whatever the product or service may be, falling behind competitors who release their version — today, if imperfectly — to the market.

Brown-vectored perfectionism is already apparently even in children. Such a child may sit down to write a poem, doing their best to make it absolutely perfect. However, the stress builds until they make a mistake right at the very end. What happens next? You can probably guess: the child grabs a clean piece of paper and starts all over again. The problem now, though, is that they are already tired and this time only make it to somewhere in the middle before another mistake crops up. The parents, running out of patience, urge the child on: "Okay, why don't we white it out? You don't have to write it again!" Not surprisingly, the child ignores their entreaties, pulls out one more clean sheet of paper, and starts over. From a distance it might look like the parents are being overly harsh to their child, but the root of the problem is that brown-vectored children can have parents who are not brown-vectored by any stretch of the imagination (it is true: regardless of genetic predispositions, we do not always carry on our parents' vectors — look for more on that in the next chapter). It is important to remember that a child like that is not necessarily putting in the work to earn a good grade at school; the internal satisfaction of knowing they did the best they could is better than any A+.

Pedantry[2], a similar quality, is also typical of the brown vector.

PROBLEMS GETTING STARTED

There is probably a point of equilibrium for everything in the

---

[2] Pedant — a person who is excessively concerned with formalism, accuracy and precision or who makes an ostentatious and arrogant show of learning.

world: brown-vectored people who are virtuosos in getting the job done (at the finish, in other words), often have issues getting over the threshold of starting. For them, beginning anything presents a difficulty that affects both everyday activities and larger-scale projects like opening a new business or getting married. The decision-making process itself is unbelievably difficult: weighing every option over and over, they consult their closest friends, read up on the subject, and constantly go back to think it all through from the beginning one more time.

Sales clerks are certainly familiar with the kind of customer who takes a long time to look over a product, reads the instructions in detail, and asks about all its finer points. Having done so, they quietly leave, only to return a couple days later and ask a few more important questions. Not all salesmen know that those — brown-vectored — people will eventually make their decision and finish what they started, finally purchasing the product that won out.

In situations like these it is almost as if brown-vectored people are waiting for some kind of shove to help them out break out of their deliberations and finally make a decision, something that explains why they so enjoy hearing advice and instructions. While they may not follow the advice, it gives them the strength they need to come to a conclusion. Try gently nudging your brown-vectored friend in one direction or another when you see him behaving like this — he will probably thank you for it later.

Brown-vectored people often drive the people around them crazy; seeing how slow they are off the blocks, many write them off as unproductive altogether. That is not the case, however: once a decision is made, brown-vectored people are more than ready to work as hard as anyone else with no further help required.

NEAT AND TIDY

Brown-vectored people are born with a powerful bent toward orderliness and cleanliness. Just like for the vector's other peculiarities, the culprit here is genetics, supplemented only to a limited degree by upbringing or lifestyle. While it may be hard to believe, there are children who shock their parents by spontaneously developing the habit of washing their hands and cleaning up after themselves. Once they hit two or three, they even start pushing the people around them to be cleaner.

A brown-vectored child might enter someone's house and immediately ask, "Where can I wash my hands?" If you were to ask their parents if they raised their child that way, they would happily tell you how tidy their home has been ever since their brown-vectored child was born.

As adults the pull toward cleanliness only grows and tightens its grip. People like this are constantly bringing up the fact that "scary" bacteria live on dirty hands and produce, causing...diarrhea! Brown-vectored people live in constant dread of diarrhea. If you are strolling around the city on a hot summer day with a friend and suggest picking up a snack from a dirty-looking street stand, you will most likely find yourself with one less friend. People with this nature tend to be very fastidious about the places they eat, though their pickiness has less to do with a refined palate: they focus more on finding tidy, hygienic restaurants staffed by immaculately dressed waiters and waitresses serving clean food. When they eat at a friend's house they often surprise their hosts with their meticulous approach to cleanliness by, for example, checking deep into the core of green onions to see if there is any dirt. The other side of that coin is that brown-vectored people do not trust anyone else to wash produce at their own houses.

Just like any other manifestation of this particular vector, the urge to be clean can become a pathology: mysophobia, or the fear of bacteria. For a reminder of how many well-known people have suffered from this disease, simply recall Leonardo DiCaprio's character in The Aviator.

I once knew someone who washed his hands four times before leaving home: first before putting on his underwear (which was perfectly clean, of course), second before putting on his shoes (to avoid staining the beautifully polished leather), third after putting on his shoes (notwithstanding, they are still worn outside), and fourth right before putting on his coat. Then he would leave his apartment, shut the door, head over to the elevator, and pull his key out of his pocket to press the button. Incidentally, in all the other areas of his life he was fairly well-adjusted and, regardless of his peculiar habits, lived a balanced life.

No less important than cleanliness is the brown-vector need for orderliness and everything that goes with it (decency, regularity, and much more). All their magazines are stacked in even rows with the face side up, and all their papers are filed in separate folders that are themselves in larger folders. The variety and functionality of the office supplies they use (different-colored pens and sharpened pencils, paper clips, staplers, daily planners, and the like) would shock you, though there is nothing superfluous in their collection of absolutely necessary tools. They love walking around office supply stores, and new supplies make great gifts for many of them.

Brown-vectored people take the same approach to outfitting

their homes and setting up their daily lives: brown-vectored homemakers work in pristine kitchens with groceries organized in labeled boxes. The cleaning supplies they use are only the latest and most ecologically efficient, while produce is cleaned, vegetables are peeled, and grains are sorted with the utmost attention to detail. Women like this love getting Tupperware and other containers as gifts, along with kitchen utensils and, most importantly, anything they can use to make their houses just a bit cleaner. Deep cleaning is not a drudgery for them; instead, it is a celebration or even something therapeutic that gets them feeling balanced and energized for quite a while. Their days begin with dusting and end with the same ritual, while the love they have for their homes as the place they can make the coziest and most comfortable has given them a reputation as ideal housewives.

Brown-vectored women do not usually get along well with housekeepers thanks to their over-anxious need for cleanliness: "How could someone else possibly have my house looking its best?!" In fact, they usually take the time to get everything spick and span themselves even after the best housekeeper they can find goes home for the day.

Brown-vectored men are known for their handiwork and thriftiness. All their tools, screws, and bolts are sorted into little boxes they label and without fail organize into larger boxes. The larger boxes are carefully set on shelves, while a detailed filing system keeps everything exactly in its place. Notice that here too there is nothing superfluous or unneeded.

Books in brown-vectored homes are evenly lined on shelves with the titles all facing a single direction, and multivolume collections are always in alphabetical or numerical order.

Sometimes everything is grouped by size, color, or some other criterion, seeing as how brown-vectored people absolutely love books: not only do they enjoy reading them, they also love buying, storing, and systematizing them.

I remember visiting a girl's house once when I was younger. She had me sit down on a couch in one room while she headed over to the kitchen to make dinner. As I sat there, I felt uncomfortable, almost as if there was something bothering my eyes. Suddenly I noticed a complete set of Encyclopaedia Britannica sitting on a bookshelf across from me. How do you think it was organized? The fifth volume was right after the first and followed by the twenty-fifth, after which were the fourth, thirteenth, and so on. How could anyone live like that?! I jumped up and sorted them numerically, somehow brightening the room in the process. When the girl return and saw my happy face, she asked, "What happened?" I proudly gestured toward the bookshelf, though she was unable to see anything different. There was no sense explaining what was going on since it would have taken a brown-vectored person to really get it.

PACKING

The pursuit of tidiness leads to outstanding packing skills, making brown-vectored people the best packers on the planet. They are so good at neatly and compactly fitting things into boxes, purses, and suitcases, in fact, that they shock the people around them by how much they can actually get inside. Needless to say, while the process takes a good while, the end result exceeds all expectations.

Many years ago I witnessed an interesting scene at an

international airport. A man ran up to security out of breath, obviously late for his plane. His suitcase was stuffed to the extent that there were things sticking out of it in a few places (we will talk about that packing style in the chapter dealing with the red vector), and just then an agent asked him to open it up. After taking his time looking through it, the inspector told the poor man, who was almost in tears, to repack the suitcase — although everything it had disgorged looked like it would fit in two suitcases. Suddenly a young man who apparently worked at the airport materialized from out of the corner and asked, "Do you need help?" "Twenty dollars," he quietly added. "Twenty dollars??!!" the man repeated, stunned. But what else could he do? The young man quietly and methodically took five minutes to pack everything into the suitcase (there was even room left over), after which the passenger handed over the money and ran off toward his plane knowing there are some things in life he will simply never be much good at.

A talent for packing is perfect for making a hobby out of collecting things. Who besides brown-vectored people could so carefully collect, describe, and systematize a wide range of items (from stamps and bottle caps to antiques and old cars)? It is true: all honest-to-goodness collectors are brown-vectored. Dmitri Mendeleev, the great "collector" and systematizer of chemical elements, serves as a great example with his side hobby of fashioning quality suitcases. Obviously, he had what it took to organize a wide range of things.

Any discussion of the meticulousness inherent to this vector would be incomplete without a mention of one more application for that quality: finances. While *thriftiness* is a key characteristic of brown-vectored people, it should not be confused with stinginess:

brown-vectored people are simply capable of coolly and prudently calculating how they spend every dollar. They are well aware of how much money they have in their account or wallet (not to the last penny, of course, but they have a good idea) and need a good reason to spend it — it takes a good, hard-working salesmen to convince them to make a purchase.

Brown-vectored people are especially careful about their food supplies. In the summer they happily stock up, rationing what they have so as to empty their shelves just in time for the following summer to roll around. Brown-vectored people also throw out food once it passes its expiration date: if you are offered jelly that expired in 1997, you can be sure your host is not brown-vectored (people who tend to have shelves loaded with expired food are orange-vectored and will be discussed in that chapter). If a chocolate bar expired yesterday, brown-vectored people are too concerned with their digestive system and overall health to eat it.

Even despite their thriftiness, brown-vectored people love entertaining guests, and for their closest friends they will spare no expense.

A MAN OF THE PAST

Brown-vectored people prefer dealing with *spent goods* in widely varying areas of their lives (Freud thought this tendency came from the brown vector's childhood love of all things bathroom-related, as bodily waste can also be considered "spent goods"). Applying that idea to *time* points the preference to the past and everything related to it. For the brown vector, the past is a brighter, happier place than the present and especially the future, which is why you may occasionally find yourself regaled by brown-vector stories of when the world was a better place. Regardless of the actual success or benefits today brings, brown-vectored people still remember yesterday (last month, last year) as being happier and better. They prize their past and everything that reminds them of it (old keepsakes or worn pictures), which is why they tend to spend a good deal of time looking back on their younger years, past loves, old jobs, and former friends. Were they to somehow gain access to a time machine, they would continually be turning the wheel backward. There is so much in life today that frustrates brown-vectored people, while the past... When tomorrow comes, however, today will take its place among the "good ol' days."

There is even a special form of psychotherapy that has proven to work well for brown-vectored people: looking over past pictures in chronological order (from birth to the present) or, even better, showing them to someone else and talking about them helps build a stable psychological foundation from which to forge a path forward into the future.

Keeping a diary makes it easy to take quick jaunts back into the past, remembering and reliving cherished memories. Brown-vectored diaries take that one step further, featuring exceptional detail that helps lock chains of events into place. Incidentally, Sigmund Freud, the originator of the vector system, kept an incredibly detailed lifelong diary — it is no coincidence that he began his description of the different character types with the brown vector. Many people, of course, try to keep diaries (some for a week, others for a month), though only the brown-vectored ones are capable of keeping up the practice regularly and over a long period of time.

This pull toward the past can also exhibit itself in a passion for history or archeology, either professionally or as a hobby (reading books or watching TV shows). Some archaeologists even call their digs "evolution's toilet."

There is no better person for anything having to do with archiving, collecting old documents, or analyzing them than a representative of the brown vector.

THE FUTURE

It is important to remember that for brown-vectored people, enamored as they are with the past, the future holds no particular interest. To take that a step further, the future for them can often be somewhat frightening: while past facts can be carefully studied, systematized, and pigeonholed, the future is a black hole of unknowns that robs brown-vectored people of their trusty psychological tools. That fact is where the characteristic brown-vector fear of everything new comes from, leaving them only accepting of new things that are really repackaged ideas from the "good old days" (a very brown-vectored phrase, by the way). If you would like to get through to someone like this with a completely new idea or sell them a new product, you will have to somehow relate it back to the past.

Brown-vectored people begin new things by doing their best to lace them with the accustomed, familiar, and proven (it is no accident that the word "recommended" is key for this vector). Often there are so many of these additives from the past that they dwarf what is actually new.

A picture of the future for brown-vectored people is made of up snapshots from experience: "Where will we go on vacation this summer? Probably where my parents used to take me…"

Brown-vectored people interested in beginning a professional relationship with a new company will be sure to look up that company's history and past experience, while new and even highly promising enterprises will be looked at askance.

Try talking with brown-vectored people about the future by making it less intimidating. Finding a reference to or analogy in the past will dramatically improve the odds of getting through to them.

Even brown-vectored children distrust everything new in their lives: it may be hard to believe, but the words "New Topic" written by a teacher on a blackboard cut brown-vector intellectual productivity by 25%. And when you really think about it, are there ever actually new topics at school? Generally everything builds on something that has come previously, and so perhaps it would be wise to stop scaring brown-vectored children with phrases like that one.

CRUELTY AND REGRET

This next tendency was withheld by Freud for good reason, as the unenlightened reader may find it to be too unattractive. Some brown-vectored people make a habit of something that can be seen as cruel: *psychological sadism.*

A brown-vectored person who thinks you are at fault about something will start pestering you with a multitude of accusations that can go on for quite a while, a period during which there is nothing you can say or do to change their mind. Even if you are already willing to admit your wrongdoing and ask how you can make up for it, the answer you receive is unequivocal: "You've done enough already." The conversation could last hours or even weeks (significantly longer for domestic relationships) without the slightest sign of progress, spoiling any kind of relationship — husband and wife, parent and child, or employer and employee. The reaction most commonly displayed by women (and children) in these situations is to simply break down and cry, which, surprising as it may seem, is actually the key to instantaneously fixing the problem. As soon as brown-vectored people see tears start to form, they instantly forget their cruelty in favor of compassion and care for their erstwhile victim. The degree to which they feel that compassion, in fact, is in direct proportion to the cruelty they previously displayed: the longer they were harsh, the longer they will regret it. Ultimately, brown-vectored sadism begins with cruelty that resolves into regret. Situations like these are much more difficult for men, for whom tears are not generally how they resolve conflicts.

Incidentally, normal sadism (the desire to inflict physical pain on another person or an animal) also originates in deep-seated and unacknowledged brown-vector needs. The pathology of this feature is excellently exhibited in the novels written by the Marquis de Sade, from whose name we get the term itself. His shocking work entitled *The 100 Days of Sodom* and the film adaptation by well-known Italian director Pier Paulo Pasolini depict the pathology of the brown vector.

It is interesting that many dentists (top-notch professionals, even) are brown-vectored with a subconscious need for their patients to feel pain. Many years ago, when anesthetics were used with much less frequency, there was a professional proverb to the effect that dentists could only do quality work if they "felt their patients' real pain." Our suffering in the chair may be nothing more than the price we pay for having a brown-vectored, and therefore highly methodical and results-oriented dentist.

The same is true for some surgeons who are unaffected by their patients' screams when being bandaged: few would want to be operated on by a surgeon who didn't have the brown-vectored habit of finishing everything they start.

Brown-vectored rapists do not kill their victims; rather than a corpse, a desire we will talk about with regards to a different vector, they need to feel their victims' pain. It so happens that brown-vectored people are generally in favor of rescinding the death penalty and replacing it with life in prison, during which criminals "pray that god would end their lives."

The link between initial pain and subsequent gain is so deeply ingrained in the brown vector that brown-vectored people often subconsciously inflict pain even on the people they love, only to later unfurl their full potential for love and tenderness.

OTHER PSYCHOLOGICAL QUALITIES

None of the other vectors are as responsible as the brown one. Brown-vectored people keep their word and are responsible to the point of sacrificing their own personal time in order to do what they say they will do. You can rely on them when push comes to shove, as they are incredibly dependable friends.

Brown-vectored employees never lie in the interests of their company, though they could never be accused of disloyalty (a brown-vectored child might answer the phone by saying, "Mommy asked me to tell you she isn't at home"). They do not take bribes and would never filch even their favorite pens or paper clips.

The same tendency can be seen behind the wheel: brown-vectored people do their best to follow all the rules, especially when it comes to speed, passing, and parking. A double line might as well be a concrete wall it would be better to not even approach — not to mention crossing! Meanwhile, 40 mph speed limits will hold them to exactly 40 mph, no matter how angry and noisy the people behind them may be. Most difficult for brown-vectored people, however, is intersections: how does the first driver in line at a red light know when to go? Getting a rolling start before the light turns green is against the law and dangerous, while waiting for green (to satisfy their conscience) means getting rear-ended... Better to not be first to begin with, so brown-vectored people let someone pass them and roll to a stop quietly and with their nerves intact.

Bringing up the rear, by the way, is a symbol of completion that characterizes the brown vector in a variety of situations in life. Tour groups will see brown-vectored people at the back picking up what others drop and doing the right thing by handing it back to its rightful owner.

Their natural honesty pushes them to fight for fairness. Even champagne is carefully and evenly poured into glasses at the first go, while no one has any reason to complain when it comes time to distribute the company's earnings.

Brown-vectored people are intelligent and capable of deep analysis as well as systematic thought. Their thought process, however, does not happen quickly, and so their sense of humor, which is directly proportional to speed of thought, is not well-developed. While brown-vectored people appreciate toilet humor as something they can relate to, they are generally uncomfortable in other situations where they only get the joke a couple minutes after everyone else has already stopped laughing. That is why they prefer to avoid groups of witty people who continually make fun of each other. Crack jokes with brown-vectored people around at your own risk.

A few years back I was teaching a course on vectors for a newspaper's editing staff (editors have to be strongly brown-vectored given the nature of their work). They all died laughing at an old and, in my opinion, not very funny joke: "For the convenience of our readers we will begin printing our newspaper without text and on toilet paper beginning next year."

Certainly, many brown-vectored propensities are looked down on in our society. A heightened interest in all things anal is clear even at an early age, while many brown-vectored needs tend to be suppressed and driven deep into the subconscious. One way or another, however, the topic surfaces in the art produced by many well-known people: take Salvador Dali, for example, and the poem in *The Art of the Fart* (part of *Diary of a Genius*, Dali's well-known book).

NEUROSIS

We now know two things to be true for people with a particularly sensitive zone: first, their predisposition is both genetic and permanent. Second, caring for a healthy organism means devoting attention to its significant zones by stimulating them to provide pleasure. Conversely, health issues can crop up when that pleasure is missing, a principle that holds true for all eight vectors. Neurosis, during which unproductive qualities replace productive ones, can also set in without enough stimulation.

For example, brown-vectored people, who generally take their time in life, in neurosis become hurried and fidgety rather than deft or efficient (in other words, qualities that are both the opposite of their norm and unproductive). Alternatively, add neurosis to brown-vectored people who are honest when in equilibrium and they will become easily discovered white liars rather than elite spies (again, opposite and unproductive qualities). Constipation turns to diarrhea, and so on.

The same occurs in stressful situations, which drive a brown-vector neurosis that is only temporary or situational. Where there is a wide range of choices (at a large store, for example), brown-vectored people sometimes feel a sudden urge to run to the bathroom that is not sickness-related at all. A similar reaction can be observed during life's other big moments, and especially during those having to do with personal relationships.

APPEARANCE AND HABITS

Brown-vectored people generally have a thick build that often features wide hips, exuding an overall sense of deep peace and firmness. While the clothes they wear may not always match, there is a certain neatness to every bit of their appearance, and the shoes they polish to a shine, their immaculately ironed shirts, and a lack of accessories all make it easy to spot them. Seeing someone carrying around two shoe brushes (one for dirt and the other for polish) is also more than enough to convince you of their strong brown vector.

Brown-vectored businessmen retie their ties — a symbol of neatness — every day (you would be somewhat wrong to think that habit characteristic of all self-respecting men: red-vectored men, for example, buy a tie when they need one, tie it once, wash it a few times, and then just throw it out).

They love wearing practical clothing and brown or other dark tones. Brown-vectored women prefer the same colors for their makeup, which they apply lightly for a clean look. Dark-colored lipstick and nail polish are also par for the course for brown-vectored women, though well-manicured nails without any polish are also a favorite. A typical hairstyle might be slicked back hair gathered in a bun for women, and anything for men that does not leave a single hair out of place. The methodical, measured approach brown-vectored people take to life plays out in their walk and other movements: they are fairly restrained and do not excessively gesticulate, with the exception of rubbing their hands together (they do this before beginning something important).

Brown-vectored people speak slowly and softly, sometimes in a monotone. A lecture taught by such a professor, for instance, might often feature drowsy or sleeping students.

Brown-vector handwriting is very clean, is easily readable, and features large letters reminiscent of squares with rounded corners (a draftsman's handwriting). Complex documents are built on a system of points and sub-points to go along with all sorts of indentations and paragraph breaks. Contracts written by brown-vectored lawyers will no doubt have a point 1.1, a point 1.1.1, and a point 1.1.1.a, all of which will be offset with a corresponding indent.

What brown-vectored people love most of all, however, is square frames and tables, both tools that ooze tidiness and orderliness. It should come as no surprise that their favorite shape is the square. With that in mind, the best way to convey information to a brown-vectored person is to use a table, no matter what the subject matter: for example, the phrase "two dogs" could be written in a table featuring all of five columns (number, description, unit of measurement, quantity, comment). Needless to say, the books that sell to people like this also offer plenty of tables.

I was once taking an exam at university. Sadly, I barely had any time to study and was only able to really learn one of the given subjects. The test covered a different one I didn't know in the least, of course, and I decided to just get up and walk away instead of wasting my time. Suddenly, however, I noticed the person giving the exam was dressed so stereotypically that it would be a crime not to try my luck. I went for broke: picking up a clean sheet of paper, I carefully drew up a table and wrote in everything I had learned the day before (information that covered a completely different topic). To be honest, I was expecting the inevitable F, but fortune happened to smile on me. The professor picked up my piece of paper and took his sweet time looking it over, though I could tell from his eyes that he wasn't reading. A minute or two of tense silence later he asked, "Did you draw this yourself?" "Of course, my ruler and pencil are right there," I answered. He took another little while to gaze at my paper, completely forgetting to compare it to the assignment, and then asked, "Would you mind if I gave you an A with no questions asked?

You've earned it if you can structure information this well." He later took my answer to show to the other professors while I trotted home with my A.

Brown-vectored people even set up their homes and work spaces in brown-colored squares: their furniture, wallpaper, curtains, and other interior decorations are likely to have square corners and fall somewhere in that color palette.

Reading and collecting instructions, be they for household appliances, furniture, or even a regular body scrub (these days all products are legally required to come with instructions), is a favorite activity of brown-vectored people. They would never dream of plugging in a new TV without first reading the instructions from cover to cover — after all, it is written right there in black and white: "Do not plug in without reading these instructions completely!" All instruction manuals are kept in a special file or box (drawer), though only for as long as the device still works. Here is where brown-vectored people diverge from orange-vectored ones, who hang on to instructions for devices they have long since thrown out. The biggest difference is with red-vectored people, however, as they do not even read directions: instead, they throw them out, thinking they are part of the packaging.

Brown-vector hobbies are likely to include sewing, knitting, embroidering, relaxed (sitting rather than sport) fishing, work around the house (brown-vectored men prefer working with wood), and writing.

LOVE AND SEX

The brown vector is one of the most reliable for any type of relationship, and to a particular degree in personal and family life. Brown-vectored people are remarkable for their faithfulness; long-term, deeply felt affection for their spouses and children; and strong sexual potential, though their natural reticence and shyness often keep those qualities hidden from the people around them. Sometimes they do not even sense or recognize their own sexuality until someone or something opens their eyes to that area of their lives.

They are fans of hugging their loved ones from *behind*, and are themselves more sensitive from that side of the body. Many brown-vectored people love a variety of anal pleasures in bed, though for others that subject remains taboo their entire lives. As a matter of fact, the more negativity a person expresses toward the topic, the stronger their brown vector.

Inflicting pain on sexual partners is also characteristic of brown-vectored people, though that can mean anything from light slaps to full-fledged sadism. Still, brown-vector sadism keeps to what is by now for us a familiar pattern: cruelty followed by regret.

Although brown-vectored people are naturally family-oriented, they still need a bit of a push even in this area. Men often need weeks to build up to the first kiss, months for sex, and years for marriage, even as they claim with complete sincerity to be seriously pondering whether or not they are ready for such a major responsibility.

Other problems occasionally crop up for brown-vectored

people even when their family life is in full swing: meeting a long-lost love, for example, can throw them into deep turmoil. Remember that many past people and events are romanticized simply because they are in the past, even while brown-vectored people deep down are completely devoted and honest. As a result, they will most likely be able to handle such a situation well, if sweating bullets the whole time. The best way out is to sit down for a chat with the object of their past affection, during the process of which the romanticized sheen will wear off and life will look completely different.

Brown-vectored people sometimes even look for a new relationship with the same eye toward the past: they are not so much trying to find someone new (with a new kind of character) as they are trying to find something familiar with a new face. "I'd like my future wife to be similar in some ways to my first love, in others to my second, and so on."

One could be forgiven for thinking that brown-vectored men and their sensitive anal orifice would always favor homosexuality. However, that would be a huge mistake, as most of them are completely heterosexual. They simply enjoy anal stimulation and other related sexual pleasures.

Certainly, homosexual men most often have a strong brown vector, though it is only one of the vectors needed to drive homosexuality. We can take a quick peek ahead by noting that the other necessary vector is the green one.

HAVING A CONVERSATION

Brown-vectored people value honesty, sincerity, and

responsibility in the people they talk with, responding well to phrases like "to tell you the truth" and "to be honest." They themselves are simply incapable of lying or deceiving, and so they have no patience for people doing the same to them. Flattery, in addition, tends to put them on edge, giving them the impression that someone is trying to pull one over on them. On the other hand, they are soothed and put in a friendly mood by conversations about the past.

Try to set goals for brown-vectored people, be they children or adults, that are broken up into clear and achievable chunks. Avoid overwhelming them with a variety of assignments, instead giving them one at a time.

"Johnny [son], you're eight years old. Soon you'll finish school, then you'll graduate from college, get your master's, and in 25 years become a professor..."

"Bill [husband], please take out the trash, wash the dishes, walk the dog, fix the toilet, play with the baby, and hang the bookshelf..."

"Peter [employee], here's what I need you to be working on for the next six months. Tonight I'll have one more project for you as well..."

All of these situations lead to a common outcome: the brown-vectored subject falls into a stupor, unable to do anything at all. The problem is that they do not see the goals set for them, or, in other words, the end of the road they are on, and cannot handle that.

"Johnny, focus on finishing second grade." Period. You can talk about his future (third grade, mind you) later.

"Bill, please fix the toilet." Period. You can ask him to do something else once the toilet is fixed.

"Peter, here's what I need you to take care of today." Period. Tomorrow you can give him the next assignment.

It may seem overly simplistic, but using sentences like these helps brown-vectored people start moving forward, maintain their mental health, and be much more productive.

Do not forget, as we have already discussed, that you cannot rush brown-vectored people. If you are trying to set something up with one of them — a date, business negotiations, or just a chat — make sure you have extra time set aside. You can be sure their natural slowness will probably make you late.

Brown-vectored people, knowing their inability to be fast or decisive, try to go through all the available options beforehand. They make plans for the future, do their best to stick to them exactly, and can be very upset when life throws them a curveball.

They usually try to leave home early when on their way to a meeting in order to avoid being late. Notwithstanding the best-laid plans, however, something always keeps them from showing up on time. For example, a simple doorway can be psychologically difficult for brown-vectored people, as doors represent a subconscious obstacle (Freud compared them to constipation, as both at their core are difficulties getting through openings). This plays out as a common behavior seen when leaving home: the person gets to the door, stops, remembers something, and turns around. They then get back to the door ready to leave, only to remember one more thing they forgot (often something not important in the least). However, as soon as they put the threshold behind them, their problems instantly disappear and they can move on in peace (this represents a difference between brown-vectored people and purple-vectored ones, who often continue worrying even after they leave home: "Did I turn off the iron? The stove?"). Long story short, brown-vectored people are often late to events regardless of their efforts to the contrary, something that really bothers them.

As you already know, this vector is not known for openness toward others, though that is true mostly in relation to strangers. Brown-vectored people happily chatter away when they are with close friends or even simply people they know — ask how your brown-vectored friend is doing at the risk of spending the next hour getting the full picture. They talk about their life in intimate detail, and are even prone to rabbit trails that eventually meander back to the main topic, which is always brought to a close.

Their meticulousness and attention to detail often makes them look boring, and there is a kernel of truth to that. A woman might find it easier to simply give the brown-vectored man what he is hinting at rather than spend an exorbitant amount of time explaining why she would rather not.

Brown-vectored people are often characterized by somewhat cyclical problems or struggles. They can spend days or weeks thinking over the same situations, sometimes continuing to mull over them even after they have made their decision.

HEALTH

When their vector's needs are met and they have reconciled themselves to its tempo and lifestyle, brown-vectored people are remarkable for their strong health. While they take a long time to do anything, they are said to also live quite a while.

People who do not understand or accept their vector (we will talk about acceptance in the next chapter) and do not provide their organism with the bodily and emotional happiness it needs can suffer from their vector's typical diseases: constipation, hemorrhoids, anal fissures, and even localized swelling. Existing statistics show that many bowel disorders and almost all rectal and anal problems are directly related to a dissatisfied or discordant brown vector. It is no accident that Germany and Japan, the countries with the strongest brown vectors, have the highest percentage of people suffering from rectal swelling.

Incidentally, intestinal dysbiosis and other stool problems suffered by both children and adults are also often related to an imbalanced brown vector.

Restoring balance for the vector results in a significant health improvement, and sometimes to complete recovery (if the disease has not gone too far, of course).

How can you help a person like this? Let's take a look at an example.

I was once reading the help column in a health magazine and noted an intriguing letter. Its unusual style drew my attention: the text was broken down into points and sub-points. It ran something like this:

"1. I am 30 years old.

2. I have suffered from constipation for 20 of them.

3. I have tried: 3.1 Herbs, 3.2 Pills, 3.3 ..." and so on.

Not doubting in the least what was causing the problem, I decided to write the poor girl a letter of my own. In it I briefly recapped the contents of this chapter, discussing how there are people for whom the anal zone is particularly sensitive from birth and how these types of diseases can result from a lack of stimulation. At the end I suggested that she try regularly massaging her anal zone with a finger or think of some other way to offer it pleasure. I had to wait for all of three months before she wrote back, but I did receive an answer:

"Doctor, thank you so much! My results:

1. The constipation is gone

2. I am happy again

3. My husband and I found a handy little trick!!!"

Please do not think that the only way of balancing the brown vector is by massaging its sensitive zone. Lifestyle, tempo, housekeeping, and favorite hobbies all play their part.

If you have a close friend or relative suffering from constipation or rectal problems, have them read this book. Simply telling them about it or giving them specific advice will not work, seeing as how it is very important for brown-vectored people to slowly digest and process information — especially something this intimate — at their own speed. Be delicate if you really want to help your brown-vectored partner.

When I was at a Viktor Tolkachev training session, one of the group participants suddenly got very emotional during the lesson on the brown vector. She cried, "Oh, that's my husband! Oh, my husband is exactly like that!" I do not know what happened in her family afterwards, but her husband drove her to the session the next day: "Keep on going to the sessions. There's something to them."

Brown-vectored women generally handle pregnancies well, though birth itself tends to be long and difficult (remember once more Freud and his "difficulty getting through openings").

PROFESSIONS

There is no one better than brown-vectored people for getting important things done, as their work meets even the strictest quality standards. As professionals, they prefer work that requires *sitting and attention to detail* (accountant, programmer, trucker); relates to the *past* (historian, archeologist, antiquity dealer, archivist, museum curator), *detailed study* (analytic, scientist), or *systematizing* things (manual or catalog author, librarian); or that has to do with *justice* (lawyer, investigator) or *cleanliness*. They also make great writers.

Brown-vectored people, as it so happens, have a natural inclination toward grammatical accuracy and can sometimes see mistakes in a text without even reading it. That should not surprise anyone, as all languages are ordered systems (regardless of their many exceptions) — brown-vectored people are born with a strong sense of order and a sharp eye for abnormalities.

In sports they love crew, horseback riding, and biking, while in medicine they generally become surgeons and dentists.

Finally, the best *teachers and educators* are more often than not brown-vectored. Brown-vectored people can build strong relationships with children by giving them what they need without spoiling them, and children love them for that.

CONCLUSION

This chapter began with a quote by Sigmund Freud (to be more precise, the first phrase in his article "Character and Anal Erotism"), so it would be logical to wrap it up with the same article's last phrase:

"We ought to consider whether other character complexes, too, do not exhibit a connection with the excitations of particular erogenous zones."

We will take up that subject in the remaining chapters. First, however, we need to discuss how a single vector can manifest itself in wildly different ways depending on the person.

FILMS TO WATCH (WITH BROWN-VECTORED CHARACTERS)

- Boxing Helena, directed by Jennifer Chambers Lynch, USA, 1993 (Nick Cavanaugh, played by Julian Sands)

- Salò, or the 120 Days of Sodom, directed by Pier Paolo Pasolini, Italy and France, 1976 (almost all characters)

Visit my site www.psy8.net to enjoy the Vector Test, the Vector Gallery (pictures, movies and citations of all eight vectors), the article about the compatibility of vectors, answers to readers' questions, and more.

Chapter 2. Defining and Accepting Vectors

As you will recall from the first chapter, the sensitivity enjoyed by each of our orifices is determined genetically. That is why the *potential* of each vector remains largely unchanged from birth straight through to the end of life. However, that is just the potential — the actual development of each vector and how they manifest themselves for each individual person across different periods of life depend on a number of factors. Two people with the same brown-vector potential may look and act completely differently, something that is impacted by more than just other vectors: the brown vector could be balanced or imbalanced for different people, for example. Beyond that, how each vector presents itself can change significantly throughout our lives. This chapter will help you navigate all of that.

You can take the Vector Test on my site www.psy8.net

The principles laid out here can be applied identically to each of the eight vectors, though, given your familiarity with the brown vector, we will use it as an example.

Scenario 1.

Imagine a child gifted from birth with a 100% brown vector (that does happen, if rarely), meaning that their brown vector potential is maximized and just about all the brown-vector qualities we have discussed could be realized. Also imagine that the child's parents are also brown-vectored (that may not be the case, as we can very easily be more similar to our grandparents than our parents in our appearance, character, or health).

This child is lucky, however, and his brown-vectored parents are as well: they can dote on a child whose character is very similar to theirs. The satisfied parents encourage him, supporting him everywhere his brown vector raises its head: "Good job sitting for so long — you'll be very diligent when you get older!" Their behavior demonstrates that they *accept* their child's brown vector completely, and the child follows in their footsteps by completely *accepting* that vector in himself and lives happily, contentedly, and harmoniously.

In this scenario the genetic potential is 100% and vector acceptance is 100%.

What kind of person will the child be when he grows up? Chances are he will be well-adjusted and healthy (note that we are only talking about this single vector at the moment), the kind of person you could look at and immediately pick up on an enormous number of easily recognizable, productive (positive) brown-vector qualities. Happily for the child, there will be no unproductive (negative) brown-vector qualities.

People who completely — 100% — accept their vector enjoy only its productive qualities.

Scenario 2.

Next imagine the same kind of child, one with strong brown-vector potential, born this time to non-brown-vectored parents. Her genes apparently skipped a generation or two, coming from her grandparents (or great-grandparents) rather than her parents. Many features and genetic diseases, incidentally, are known to take that generational or bi-generational leap.

With that said, the child's parents are simply wonderful, loving her with all their hearts despite the fact that her character is in many ways dissimilar to theirs. They accept her for who she is, although they do not necessarily encourage her brown vector when it manifests itself. All said, the parents accept her brown vector for the most part, though not 100% (perhaps something like 80%), and as a result the child accepts her own brown vector at that same solid level of 80%.

What kind of person will this child grow up to be? Well-adjusted and healthy overall, it will be fairly easy to tell that she is brown-vectored. While maybe not visible immediately, it will still be clear thanks to being fairly well-endowed with brown-vector qualities. Will there be any unproductive brown-vector qualities? Yes, though not very many, an outcome that is more often encountered in real life than the first.

Scenario 3.

We start from the same position: a child is born with significant brown-vector potential. However, his parents are anti-brown, as they both are not brown-vectored personally and despise the brown-vectored people around them.

And what luck! Practically everything about their child drives them crazy: how methodical he is, how hung up he gets on insignificant details, how long he sits on the potty. Not only do they consider those qualities bad or even unhealthy, they may be ashamed of the way their child acts or think there is something wrong with him. The parents do everything in their power to retrain their child and modify his behavior: "What's taking so long? Let's go! Come on! Stop washing your hands! You waste so much water!" As a result, the child's natural behavior is repressed and eventually forgotten, *roughly crammed into his subconscious.*

The parents' acceptance of their child's brown vector in this case is minimal (say, 30%), and the child follows in their footsteps by feeling ashamed of what makes him who he is. He tries instead to be someone else and in so doing earn his parents' approval. As a result, he does his best not to act from within himself, but to conform to the significant adults around him. The effort the child exerts is so strong that eventually he is successful: every year more and more productive brown-vector qualities go into hiding. But what happens with unproductive qualities? Let us take a look at a simple model to see what happens to the existing potential.

Imagine a rubber blow-up rabbit. It has a body, two pairs of legs, a head, ears, and a little tail, all of which look well-balanced and symmetrical absent defects. For the sake of experiment, we can try squeezing one of its paws — the air is pushed into other body parts that in turn expand. Next we tie off the deflated paw so that it nearly disappears and move on to the next one. We can imagine, watching the air from the second paw transfer elsewhere, what would happen if we did the same with a third paw, an ear, and a tail: the rabbit would morph into an unrecognizable blob with a few oversized appendages. Nobody would be able to tell that those appendages were a leg, an ear, and a head.

The blow-up rabbit models an individual vector (any of them), rather than a complete person. Genetic potential is not redistributed between vectors; instead, it is pushed between a single vector's qualities.

That potential is distributed evenly at birth. Parents and later people on their own who accept a specific vector allow it to develop harmonically and proportionally, with all its qualities productive and none "overinflated" or "underinflated." On the other hand, if a vector is only accepted to a low degree, meaning that the parents and person do their best to suppress some of its natural manifestations, the vector's other qualities are proportionally "overinflated." That end result is always unproductive.

For example, brown-vectored people are always slow and methodical. If the brown vector is balanced (completely accepted), their slowness will be both appropriate and productive. Such a person would be able to slowly but inexorably churn their way through quite a few things, if at a slower pace, while those around them flit from one to the other. However, if the vector is out of balance ("overinflated" like that blow-up rabbit's appendages), that same slowness is counterproductive and becomes a hindrance.

A brown-vectored person is concentrating on a math test she is taking. She is obviously trying to push herself to go faster, since she has been told more than once that she is dawdler watching life pass her by. Sadly, her efforts to speed things along seem to have the opposite effect, and soon the teacher comes over: "Hurry up! The bell's going to ring soon, and you're still working on the first problem!" With that, the student's thought process is irrecoverably lost.

But what happened? It appears the child has an unaccepted brown vector, otherwise she would not have been so slow. The teacher, in her effort to get a move on things, only added to the pressure exerted on the unaccepted brown-vector qualities (going back to our model, the teacher is squeezing those rabbit appendages just a little harder), resulting in the child's excessive slowness, an unproductive quality, becoming even more pronounced.

What could the teacher have done differently? Perhaps she could have walked over and quietly mentioned, "Relax, there's still time left. You do a better job when you aren't hurrying." That way she would have expressed her acceptance of the child's brown vector and let her stop worrying about how slow she was going (in other words, let her accept her own vector). As a result, the work would have been done faster and better, at the child's natural pace.

Working quickly means slow movements made one right after the other (a brown-vector saying).

Generally speaking, balanced people (those for whom all their existing vectors are accepted) do not have unproductive qualities. All unproductive or, as they are often called, negative qualities are driven by suppressed features of a vector that exaggerate others, just like with the blow-up rabbit.

What is the point of discussing all of this? And what can a person do who sees an overwhelming number of unproductive qualities in himself and those around him?

We can use the exact same model to answer that question. If we find a blow-up rabbit in that pitiful condition (remember that at the end it looked like some kind of blob with a few engorged appendages), we first need to figure out what is suppressed (finding those areas can be anything but simple, since those tied-off nubs are miniscule next to the giant rabbit). Then we need to untie them. What happens next? The air in the rabbit settles back into the newly created space and soon the rabbit looks just like it did when it was "born," with balanced limbs and features. How much time that takes depends on how long the rabbit was in that state, meaning that untying recently tied-off limbs could get things back to the status quo in a matter of hours or days. On the other hand, if it lived a good while tied-off and misshapen, it might take weeks or months before the material can remember and get back to the way it used to be.

The same is true of suppressed vectors. If you find unproductive traits of a particular vector in yourself, you need to figure out which other qualities have been suppressed — perhaps by close adults, life itself, psychological trauma, or something else (incidentally, just understanding the problem goes a long way toward resolving it).

Then you can use the tool that works best: *acceptance*, or the equivalent of untying the blow-up rabbit's nubs. By accepting your vector, you allow it to find a balance that minimizes unproductive qualities (overinflated limbs) and maximizes the productive qualities you have always had.

You can do the same for other people, and especially your loved ones. If you find unproductive qualities in your child or another adult, you can still bring *acceptance* to bear. Accept that vector as a whole, even with its unproductive qualities, which will release the person to accept it for themselves. The result will not keep you waiting.

Once at a training seminar a brown-vectored women could not get over the fact that her young adult daughter could never remember to make her bed (we can jump ahead and note that the daughter was strongly red-vectored). Even after quite a few lessons the woman could not understand how acceptance was important to her situation. At the second-to-last lesson she once again raised the issue and, after I gave her a detailed answer, sat in thought for a while. Then, at the last lesson, she was simply shining: "You know, I was on my way home last time and suddenly understood what acceptance means. It was like something dawned on me right there in the metro! But you know what is most surprising? I got home and my daughter's bed was already made — for the first time without anyone yelling!"

That is how accepting vectors in other people works: often instantaneously and miraculously. From that example we can see that acceptance is less an action and more an attitude.

Acceptance means relating to how your or someone else's vector displays itself with no evaluation whatsoever (not judging good from bad) and giving it room to exist for no other reason than because it is already in your or that person's life. Even beyond that, acceptance is acknowledging that nothing manifests itself in a person senselessly: all qualities are there for a reason and serve some purpose, even if the how and why are not apparent.

Some might object: "So what, I just have to be happy about my negative qualities and everything will be fine??" No, it is not about being happy; it is about acceptance, or relating to them *without making any kind of judgment.*

When we accept a vector and all the qualities that come with it, including the unproductive ones, it balances and the unproductive qualities disappear.

The opposite of acceptance is exclusion. That can be passive, by simply "forgetting" that an unpleasant quality or habit exists, or it can be active, which is when someone actively struggles with something they do not like in themselves or someone else. The problem is that a battle with one's own manifestations (in other words, with one's self) cannot be won, and only drains time and energy.

Now let's go back to the different ways a vector can develop.

Scenario 4.

The genetic potential is 60-70%, while the parents accept it completely. A person like this would grow up healthy and balanced, given the 100% acceptance. They would be much less reminiscent of a pure brown vector than in scenario two, though 70% is still pretty significant. At the end of the day, it would take just a brief conversation to see that brown vector peeking out.

Scenario 5.

The genetic potential is 10-20%, meaning that the child can really not be called brown-vectored at all. She will have very few brown-vector characteristics, though her parents accept them fully and she grows up healthy and balanced. Note that there are many non-brown-vectored people in the world, and they can be just as successful and happy as anyone else. Also note that in this situation we are talking about a fully accepted vector, weak though it may be.

Scenario 6.

The genetic potential is the same 10-20% as in the last example, though "brown-vectored monsters" is too soft a term for the parents. They are fully convinced that the most important qualities in life are sitting still, being thorough, and being thrifty, though their child, as if on purpose, is born completely bereft of those traits. Well, good thing they studied all those books on how to raise children (do you remember how brown-vectored people love books?)! They are now ready to wield their arsenal of child-rearing tips and tricks to make their child act the way they think he should.

Children who are born with weak brown-vector potential will stay that way, meaning it is impossible to make them brown-vectored. Certainly, they may be able to force themselves to display different brown-vector traits, though those traits will have nothing to do with the vector itself; instead, they mean the children in some situations act as they were taught by their parents. Sometimes that can look very odd:

A friend of mine could not have been further from the brown vector, though his parents did their best to make him brown-vectored. One thing important to his brown-vectored mother was washing the apples they always had around the house from their giant apple tree. As a child, however, my friend had no problem picking an apple up off the ground and eating it with no second thought given to his health. His mother did her best to raise him well, and after a few years she had reached her goal: for the rest of his life he reflexively washed apples before eating them.

I once invited him over and asked him to wash a basket of fruit. On his way to the sink he dug through the apples on top, grabbed a dirty pear from the bottom, and ate it without blinking an eye. A couple minutes later he bit into a beautifully cleaned apple. That is how a trained, situational reflex works as opposed to an innate need for cleanliness.

Scenarios 3 and 6 often occur for a particular parenting style, though within the context of different vectors. As a result, what children should naturally display at birth is suppressed and replaced by something artificial and unnatural. They accustom themselves to behaving how their parents or other significant adults want them to, in the process losing touch with who they really are. In fact, it is excruciatingly difficult and often impossible for them to differentiate between their own qualities (their natural vectors) and those they acquired when they were young. They very well may claim unnatural values to be their own with complete sincerity, push toward unnatural goals they think are their own, and ultimately come away with nothing but dissatisfaction in widely varying areas of their lives. When a person lives someone else's life, they waste an incredible amount of energy forcing their life away from their personal calling, real success, real love, and real happiness. Does that sound familiar?

The most important thing you should learn from this book is probably how to understand what part of you is really you and what part is not (you can also learn to make this distinction for other people). Simply thank that foreign part (it has been with you for a while, after all) and start living life differently: in line with your innate vectors.

ONE MORE THING

It is crucial to understand that vector acceptance, unlike genetic potential, can change to a large degree over the course of a lifetime, ranging from 0% to 100%. In childhood that number depends on significant adults (family members, teachers, other educators), while adults are responsible for it themselves.

Parents and other significant adults are responsible for accepting children's vectors. Adults, on the other hand, must accept their own.

Of course, children can be so psychologically traumatized that they cannot recover even as adults, at least independently. That, however, is an exception to the rule. For the most part, we as adults control vector acceptance ourselves, which is the key to resolving most of the problems we face in our relationships (with ourselves and those around us), our personal development, our health, and other areas of our lives.

Some of you are probably wondering if all you have to do is resign yourself and be indifferent to everything that happens. Absolutely not!

Acceptance is not indifference or resignation. Rather, it is a mental act that requires a certain amount of effort put forward while always hoping for improvement. Indifference holds no hope for the future and takes no energy, while resignation has more to do with hopelessness. Let me illustrate:

An overweight young woman walks up to her mirror in the morning:

Resignation: "Still a fat old cow. Awful! Well, nothing I can do about it... Looks like I'll be an old maid... I'll think I'll go have a snack to cheer me up..." She slouches away from the mirror with tears in her eyes and a week later has gained three more pounds.

Indifference: "Still fat and ugly. Time to get back to my dissertation." She steps away from the window thinking about her dissertation and a week later nothing has changed.

Acceptance: "It would be nice to lose a few pounds, but even with the extra weight I am beautiful and successful. I think I'll go meet somebody new." She bounces away from the mirror with a shining face and a week later has lost three pounds.

Fighting one's self: "That's it! I can't live like this! Tomorrow I'm starting some kind of strict diet until I lose twenty pounds!" A week later she has lost ten pounds, though her head and liver hurt, her face is haggard, her sex drive is missing in action, and her life is bereft of happiness. Someone may have won that battle with herself, but it is obvious that someone has definitely lost...

This example is certainly a bit contrived, though I hope it

shows one thing: acceptance does not mean that development has stopped. Instead, it drives development toward positive change. Resignation, on the other hand, is characterized by the phrase, "Nothing I can do about it…"

THE RECIPE FOR ACCEPTING UNPRODUCTIVE QUALITIES WITHIN ANY VECTOR

Recognize that IT (a quality) exists.

When possible, make no moral judgment as to whether IT is good or bad — IT simply is.

Understand that if IT exists, it came from somewhere and serves a purpose(!).

Give IT space in your life just because IT is already there.

Understand that excluding IT (forgetting or struggling with IT) can only make IT stronger and more unproductive.

Understand that only acceptance (all of the above) can make IT really insignificant, such that IT no longer bothers you and is easily integrated into your productive life.

Replace the pronouns with a particular quality or habit of yours that you do not like and read those six points again.

ABOUT THE VECTOR TEST

Our vector test has results displayed in two diagrams. The eight rows in the first show the potential innate to each of the eight vectors, while the eight in the second reflect the acceptance those vectors currently enjoy.

What result should you have to be successful and happy? Training seminar participants often answer that question in a number of different and interesting ways: "The best is when all of your vectors have 100% potential!" "It's better when the potential for all your vectors is the same." "It would work well to have the acceptance equal the potential, for example 50% and 50%." However, all those answers are wrong.

A person can be completely developed on a personal level, successful, and happy with any combination of vectors (the upper diagram), while that can only be true if they fully accept what they are naturally given (the lower diagram).

People with high potential in seven or eight vectors can of course blossom into widely varying areas. On the other hand, it is much more common to see strong potential wasted than it is to see more moderate potential wasted. That may be due to excessive ambition; it may also occur because people with sky-high potential in different areas jump back and forth between them without ever finding what they personally enjoy most of all.

Many readers here will raise an important point: "How can you measure genetic potential using a psychological test?" While this test does not analyze your genes, it is based on the study of tens of thousands of people, with the questions and algorithm behind the results thoroughly vetted and proven. Regardless, attempting to measure psychology (or genetics) mathematically is "magic" to a certain degree, and so you would do well to take your results with a grain of salt.

CHAPTER 3. THE RED VECTOR — URETHRA

WHO'S THE BOSS?

This chapter will discuss a vector that is in many ways the complete opposite of the brown vector. Its sensitive zone (orifice) is the urethra as well as the entire urogenital system, which is why Viktor Tolkachev referred to it as the "urethral" vector.

You can take the Vector Test on my site www.psy8.net

Red-vectored people particularly enjoy both urination and drinking large amounts of fluids, while their unusually sensitive reproductive organs make them incredibly active sexually.

We will dive into all the characteristics of red-vectored people, but first we should take a look at a fascinating fact directly related to this vector.

There is an interesting substance called *uric acid* contained in our blood, muscles, and internal organs. Some people have much more of it than others, something scientists have long known is determined genetically. Crucially, uric acid exerts a powerful influence on our character: those with more of it tend to be more active and prefer leadership roles in society.

(Interesting fact: the alphas in charge of monkey troops in the wild have much higher levels of uric acid than their compatriots! That

information will come in handy, as it is much easier to study many instinctive features of the red vector in the context of ancient societies.)

On the other hand, it is equally well-known that higher levels of uric acid in the body can lead to gout (a condition caused by uric acid crystallizing and forming deposits in inflamed and painful joints). We can put two and two together, remembering that many of the great rulers of the past suffered from gout (Peter the Great, Ivan the Terrible, Benjamin Franklin, Oliver Cromwell, and others).[3]

I bring this up to show that urethral sensitivity and the amount of uric acid our bodies contain are linked genetically! It so happens that people who enjoy drinking and urinating large quantities of liquids tend to be leaders and "alphas"[4] who push their way to the front of the line in all aspects of their lives.

Many qualities inherent to the red vector, including selflessness and altruism, are derived from that propensity to take charge of other people. Yes, red-vectored people are honest-to-goodness altruists — their main concern, after all, is the survival and progress of their "herd," be that their family, company, team, or any other group. They are prepared to sacrifice everything for

---

[3] It is interesting to note that gout is one of the oldest diseases known, having been written about by Hippocrates. Some of humanity's best minds have suffered from it, including the ancient philosophers Achilles and Oedipus, Alexander the Great, Cardinal Mazarin, Michelangelo, Guy de Maupassant, Stendhal, Columbus, Newton, and Charles Darwin. Geneticists have even identified genes linked to gout.

[4] The imagery of red-vectored people as the "alphas of the herd" originated with Viktor Tolkachev and will be used throughout this chapter.

the sake of the lives and success of those people, even at the cost of their own.

With that said, while that same red-vectored person may be an altruist where the big picture is concerned, he is ego-centric when it comes to the details. Judge for yourself: can a leader responsible for the lives and success of a large group afford to think about every person in that group individually? Probably not, and there is no blame in that. The leader is well-equipped to manage situations from the top down in other areas of life as well, while still leaving the details to others. A disregard for individuals is therefore a common trait of the red vector, with red-vectored people behaving cynically with the big picture in mind and pursuing their goals practically on the backs of those around them. Firms in crisis that are managed by such a person are sure to survive, though some individual employees will pay for that survival with their careers...

As you will remember from the last chapter, vectors that are accepted to a high degree only manifest unproductive qualities minimally. A strongly red-vectored manager, therefore, who has accepted her own vector is able to stoop to the level of even the lowest employee, a habit exemplified by the great politicians and businessmen of the past (Dale Carnegie's book *How to Win Friends and Influence People*[5] is littered with examples).

---

[5] *How to Win Friends and Influence People*, published in 1936 and currently available in many languages around the world, is Dale Carnegie's most well-known book. It is a collection of practical tips and actual examples from the lives of successful people.

FROM FIRE TO INGENUITY

The fast-paced red-vector life makes it imperative that the entire body and especially brain are humming along at light speed, something that is facilitated by a unique system: *"hot"* or *"explosive"* biochemistry. Red-vectored bodies are really very warm — it is almost as if they are burning up inside, which makes it no surprise that for them fire is a symbol of internal interaction. They are the kind of people who can stare at a burning flame for hours, while as children they can think of no better pastime than setting things on fire.

If their passion for fire is taken to a professional level, they become firemen or pyrotechnicians.

Red-vectored people sometimes have a higher body temperature (98.6° to 99.5°) at which they feel perfectly normal. In fact, it would be reasonable to say that unneeded energy is converted to heat via the well-known law of physics. On the other hand, however, that temperature drops to a more normal range without resorting to medicine or any other form of treatment whenever red-vectored people find something they can pour their energy into. Their favorite color is often bright red, while their favorite shape is the symbol of fire: triangles. You may remember that person on every hike who sits by the campfire longer than anyone else, watching as it burns itself out and finally dousing it by doing something else he enjoys.

The character exhibited by red-vectored people is also reminiscent of fire or even an explosion: they are highly active, emotional, and impulsive. Finding it difficult to do the same thing for a long time, they instead prefer multitasking. For example, they read multiple books at the same time without even bothering to start at the beginning; jumping in at the middle or the end lets them find out how the story ends much faster. A business with a person like this at the helm will be working on two or three projects at the same time, often in widely differing industries. The boss himself can be seen talking into two phones simultaneously while at the same time dictating something to his secretary and giving instructions to his assistant.

Important decisions are made in the same way. The red vector, as opposed to the brown vector, rarely takes the time to carefully think through different options; instead, it instantly grasps the situation and is prepared to make a move. It is almost as if there are multiple computer processors all running at the same time — the answer is ready before the question has even been asked.

Imagine a little red-vectored boy at his school desk. The teacher slowly winds her way through a boring question: "There are ten apples... hanging on an apple tree... Seven of them... fall to the ground..." "Three!!!" the boy happily cries, having quickly grasped the question. But what does he get for his trouble? "Bobby, sit quietly until I finish asking the question!" But just sitting there is so boring, and the boy finds something else to do while the teacher continues: "Seven of them... fall to the ground... Here's the question: ... How many apples... are left on the tree? Okay, Bobby, now you can answer." By now, however, red-vectored Bobby has already figured out five similar problems and completely forgotten what the teacher is working on with the rest of the class. "Oh, so you don't know?! You get a D so you'll remember not to interrupt next time when you don't know anything."

Does that sound familiar? It is how one of the brightest students in the class can end up a C student and lose interest in studying altogether. That C has nothing to do with what the student has learned; on the contrary, it is the average of D's (when she was too fast or slow) and A's (when she happened to find a happy medium). Teachers often conclude that such students are "smart, though they need to apply themselves..."

You can probably guess that this vector does not make for great students, though "advanced" red-vectored people are still capable of impressing those around them with their unusual education. After holding an intelligent, in-depth discussion of any topic for five minutes — on politics, economics, science, art, or anything else — the conversation is so gripping and energetic that people are left wondering, "Wow, such a smart, educated person! It's a shame she had to run off so quickly..." And why did she? Well, she had nothing left to talk about.

Red-vectored people's strengths would never make for good Jeopardy contestants; while they lack breadth or depth of knowledge, they can sift through a flood of information and quickly grasp what is important. There are many examples of red-vectored people whose tremendous success was not hindered by dropping out of university: Bill Gates (Microsoft), Steve Jobs (Apple), Mark Zuckerberg (Facebook), and others.

The life of a red-vectored person is a rollercoaster of steep ups and equally steep downs. At their peak, what they churn out would take ten other-vectored people ten years to accomplish, while their valleys are bereft of energy to the point that they have no desire to do anything whatsoever.

Watch as a red-vectored child runs, jumps, and shouts like a whirling dervish until suddenly dropping everything to collapse onto the couch. Then see how his mother walks over to drone over him, "I won't give you anything until you put all your toys away *carefully and put the boxes on the shelves*." But the boy is too tired to even object, so what happens?

Teenagers are past masters of pulling batteries out of a dead MP3 player and smacking them together to squeeze out a few more minutes. The same is true of the red-vectored boy: it is absolutely possible to pick him up off the couch and make him do what his mom wants, though doing that too often will lead to some unpleasant consequences. Just like those batteries need some time to recharge, the red-vectored boy needs some peace and quiet right then to get his own batteries going again. Until that happens, he will lay there exhausted — something we usually call laziness. However, it is not just laziness; the boy simply has no energy left and needs to recharge. How long might that last? It is different every time and for every person, sometimes taking an hour, other times a day, a month, or a year. Occasionally it even takes the rest of a person's life, as illustrated by well-known scientists and artists who are never quite able to follow up their *magnum opus* with something equally as creative and consuming.

In other words, pestering red-vectored people at a time like that may not be the best idea. If you have the interests of your husband, employee, or child at heart, you will give them all the time they need to recharge. Do so and you will later find them more than willing to get everything done — and able to do so even faster.

A PERSON OF THE FUTURE

Leaders who care about their team (family, company, and so on) often give thought to tomorrow, the day after, and even the distant future. Red-vectored people are rooted in what comes next, driven toward it and drawn by the promise of new ideas and grandiose plans.

While brown-vectored people are enamored by the past's known facts and figures (they can be lined up, accumulated, systematized, organized, and drawn to a conclusion), nobody knows what will happen in the future. Moving to that side of the timeline, the only finality in the future for red-vectored people is death. Yes, you read that correctly: any point in the future that represents a conclusion is death! That is why they feature another fascinating psychological trait: no matter how many projects they start, they never finish any of them.

This is true in both little and big things: while red-vectored women can wash a mountain of dirty dishes, there will always be at least one plate left in the sink when they walk away. Maybe the phone rang, maybe their TV show started, or maybe they just got tired of washing dishes — the reason does not matter. Red-vectored entrepreneurs can get any number of projects off the ground, but they will never complete any of them (on their own, at least). This may be the key to what makes red-vectored businessmen good managers: they begin things and hand them off to others to finish (some brown-vectored colleagues, for instance). Incidentally, brown-vectored people make ideal assistants for red-vectored leaders, both finishing things and serving as a buffer between management and labor.

Intrigued as they are by the future, red-vectored people cannot stand anything having to do with the past — history, past experiences (especially those of other people), the word "recommended," and so on. They do not listen to anyone, they learn from their own mistakes, and they enjoy finding themselves in uncharted territory. We should take a moment to note here that red-vectored people learn from their mistakes instantly and do not repeat them, in contrast to many of the other vectors.

It is almost as if red-vectored people were created by nature to handle life's toughest situations without the benefit of time or resources. When it comes to their ordinarily lives they make a habit of laying on the couch as long as possible, only jumping up in time to get everything done at lightning speed and at the last possible minute. That is how they squeeze the most enjoyment out of life; doing things slowly and surely (the brown-vector way) is not their cup of tea.

Red-vectored people generally dislike reading historical books, finding it boring to waste time on what happened a long time ago. Adventures, detective stories, and fantasy, on the other hand, give them invaluable ideas for their creative pursuits.

FIRST IN LINE

An important characteristic of the red vector is a thirst for first place — after all, alphas by definition are always out in front. A motto for them could be something like "better dead than second," as they always want to be at the front of the line. If that position has already been taken, however (for example, if someone has already entrenched themselves as the leader), red-vectored people instantly lose interest. Willpower and endurance, after all, do not generally characterize this kind of person, which is why they often find excuses for their overreaches: "Oh, I didn't really want it anyway."

If your red-vectored child knows the math champion is in the next class over, she will most likely not study math at all: "Why study if you can't be first?" Instead, she will only do her best where she has the opportunity to end up alone at the front of the pack, be that as a student or a troublemaker. That is why red-vector buyers often fall for conniving salesmen who sell them on being first or acquiring an exclusive product or service. All VIP privileges, elite status, and other hooks are designed with the sole purpose of reeling in red-vectored people.

Naturally, relegating a person like this to an assistant position is highly dangerous, as they will fight for the top of the totem pole even at the cost of the whole team's work. They are also not built to be worker bees; instead, they are more comfortable thinking up new ideas, delegating them to others, and laying back while their plans are brought to fruition. After all, there are few things more relaxing than watching a burning flame, running water, or people working — a perfect description of the red vector. Others, on the other hand, may act much differently: brown-vectored people (as well as black- and orange-vectored ones) simply have to work if someone else around them is, demonstrating that all sayings and even life principles only fit certain vectors.

By the way, about that "running water" — just like fire, for this kind of person it is a symbol of Life. Their particularly sensitive urethra means urinating is especially enjoyable for red-vectored babies, and any running liquid is enough to have them in throes of delight from a young age. Leaving this kind of child in the bathtub alone means a visit from your downstairs neighbors, since there is no way the child will be able to keep the water inside the tub. Dress her up in a clean, new outfit when the weather has been clear and sunny for weeks and she will find and jump headlong into the only dirty puddle for miles around. Water sports and professions that keep them near the water are favorites for adults, who also enjoy water-related hobbies. Beyond that, something will always be running in the background — pipes, faucets, ball and feather pens…

Their struggle for first place drives red-vectored people as they find their way in life and go about their jobs. They always find unbeaten paths and love experimenting: "we'll find another way" is a favorite pronouncement. Be careful when giving one of them advice or you may involuntarily give them reason to doubt their superiority, a serious blow to their self-esteem. Deep down red-vectored people think that following someone's advice means they are no longer the smartest person in the room, and losing that title is the worst thing that could possibly happen. With that in mind, tread lightly when offering advice and do not be surprised if your idea is later regurgitated with no mention of you, the original author.

This is linked to an inability to admit to mistakes, as red-vectored people one way or another pass the blame on to those around them. After all, an admission of guilt would mean, at least to red-vectored people, an instant topple from their pedestal. Recall *The Jungle Book* and Mowgli's "Akela missed!" Who is the alpha now?

If a red-vectored person dumps the blame on you, do not feel bad: you did nothing wrong, he just does not know any better. Try to take the high road and let it roll off your back, an attitude that will be rewarded a thousandfold. On the other hand, trying to prove your innocence and shift the blame back to where it belongs will not leave you satisfied either — your red-vectored friend will never admit to being in the wrong, and your relationship will be ruined. People like this also respond aggressively to accusations, losing productivity and quite possible falling into red-vectored neurosis (we will discuss that topic soon).

Of course, if the red vector is sufficiently accepted, the person is able to own up to his mistakes and even do so publically with unusual dignity. Nobody will understand, however, what that admission costs.

RISK AND INSECURITY

If there is one peculiarity red-vectored people do their best to hide and the people around them do not even suspect, it is a hidden insecurity complex. Every morning people like this wake up with a subconscious question on their mind: "Am I really willing to give up my life for the herd?" In an attempt to prove to themselves and those around them that they really are, they never miss a chance to show their bravery: going skydiving or bungee jumping; walking under overhangs without anything to keep them safe; skiing, driving, or riding their motorcycles as fast as they can; and so on. They choose the riskiest professions and hobbies (pilots, mountain climbers, stuntmen), and their lives are spent constantly flirting with death. "Nothing ventured, nothing gained" is a motto for all aspects of life, and adrenaline rushing through their veins is the biggest thrill on earth. That is why red-vectored people rarely die in their own homes; they generally fall prey to explosions, accidents, catastrophes, falls...

From childhood they feel a strong pull toward weightlessness or freefall, seeing as how their most sensitive system is their vestibular apparatus. Maybe you are wondering what the connection is between the urogenital system and that particular apparatus, one that is located deep within the inner ear? Just think about where you get butterflies when on a high-speed elevator or traveling quickly across steep hills or small bridges. They start fluttering around near the bottom of your stomach — for women in the uterus and for men in the prostate. It turns out we sense g-forces and weightlessness with our inner ear, while we feel them far away in our urogenital organs.

Red-vectored people not only pursue risk in the form of extreme sports; they also approach business in the same way, balancing on the line between big-time success and abject failure. Their fascination extends only as far as the stakes are high, meaning they also tend to enjoy high-stakes gambling and life-and-death games.

FREEDOM

As you may have already guessed, the most important thing in the life of a red-vectored person is freedom. They would never submit to anyone, and their own system is always better than anyone else's. Do not even think about disciplining them, as red-vectored children often announce to their parents something to the effect of, "I'm going to do what I want to do, no matter what." It is no accident that children like that often run away from home, especially if they have strict parents.

I remember once when I was eight a friend from school and I decided to have a little adventure. After asking people passing by for a little money, we bought tickets for our local suburban train and set off. Once onboard, we decided to get off at a tiny little station in the middle of an open field that did not even have a real name — it was called "19 Mile Outpost." The platform was much shorter than the train and we guessed the wrong car to be in, so we had to jump straight onto the ground. My friend hesitated by the open doors (his brown vector was obviously making itself heard), though I quickly "helped" him make up his mind and jumped down behind him. The doors closed and the train chugged away...

That was the first time I was enveloped by that indescribable feeling of freedom, and I still remember it — the endless field, the rails, the receding train, and not a soul for miles. Once we had our fill of the new sensation we decided to head back, though once we got to the other side of the tracks we learned that the train only stopped at that station once every three hours. Now would be a good time to mention the main circumstance of our adventure: it was winter, the temperature had dropped to 15-20 degrees below freezing, and we were dressed more for a short trip in a warm train than for a long walk across a snowy field. I will not describe how we tried to flag down all the trains passing by, including freight trains, for three hours. Suffice it to say our train finally arrived as it was beginning to get dark and we were soon home. Of course, my brown-vectored parents had a field day with their "teaching moment," but I remember it for a completely different reason: it was the first time I felt what it means to be Free.

There are no obstacles in the life of a red-vectored person, as the word "permission" is not in their vocabulary and minor inconveniences only stir them on to try harder. They say you have to trick children like this into doing what you want: "Tomorrow you're going to school." "No, I'm not!" "Tomorrow you aren't going to school." "What are you talking about? Of course I am!" This well-known strategy works both on children and to a large degree on many adults, as telling them not to do something is a sure-fire way to achieve the opposite effect. It is much better to allow them something (or at least not to force them), causing them to lose interest in what is no longer forbidden fruit.

Red-vectored people accept nothing that infringes on their freedom. In fact, they do their best to avoid anything that even symbolizes a lack of freedom, things like items that form an enclosed circle: a tie around their neck, a buttoned top button, or a wedding ring on their finger. Some red-vectored people even prefer to keep wristwatches in their pockets, while registrations and other official documents are also considered symbols of a lack of freedom.

Strict work schedules can sometimes make red-vectored people completely unproductive. They need more flexibility, something that is most often available for those working for themselves. Everything that infringes on their freedom feels like a trap they do their best to free themselves from as soon as possible.

The most unpleasant trap for red-vectored men is when a woman comes up to them saying, "Dear, we're going to have a baby!" The first thing they think is, "Hold on a second, dear, aren't *you* the one who's going to be having the baby?!" If the next thing they hear is "...and *you have* to take care of it!", that baby may very well grow up without a father. The problem is that the *sense of duty* for red-vectored people shackles them, and the phrase "you have to" will always knock them for a loop. They love repeating something like, "I will never have to do anything for anyone!" With that in mind, women who would like to marry a red-vectored man should avoid starting that marriage with a pregnancy.

So what should a woman in that situation do? Sometimes the simplest option is the best: "Dear, the baby is yours, but you'll never see it!" There are a lot of effective elements in a phrase like that: reverse psychology, a restriction (limiting freedom, in other words), and taking away that all-important red-vector herd and future. Often that is all it takes to goad the father into taking care of the child with a level of attention that surprises those around him...at least until he hears a casual "you have to..."

Freedom is a kind of fertilizer for the red vector. If there is not enough of it in a red-vectored person's life, she will start looking for imaginary freedom in alcohol, narcotics, or virtual reality. We should note that unfulfilled red-vectored people have an affinity to alcoholism that goes beyond other vectors. That condition also serves as evidence of when the vector is not at all accepted: red-vector neurosis.

If a red-vectored person is not in charge of her herd, she becomes a lone wolf — after all, they dislike working for other people. Regardless, a balanced and fulfilled red-vectored person will always find and take charge of a herd.

People like this are unaccustomed to submitting themselves to widely accepted norms and set rules; they are inveterately suspicious of all moral principles forced on them by others. Sometimes they even want to reach all the way to the bottom in order to get a better grip on the fullness of life, going through all the depths and heights it has to offer in order to come away with a richer, fuller experience.

It is important to remember that a passion for freedom is not the same thing as irresponsibility. Quite the contrary: mature, balanced red-vectored people (for whom the red vector is accepted) are more often than not very responsible in the areas of their lives they choose. Of course, that is not true of situations where there is external pressure to be responsible.

With that in mind, the irresponsible behavior of red-vectored children striving to achieve some measure of freedom is nothing more than immaturity and imbalance that is actually natural to all red-vectored people regardless of their age.

This kind of person often needs some compliments or even flattery (another form of fertilizer for the red vector, incidentally) to get themselves going. While you can only praise brown-vectored people for something they have actually done without making them feel like a fool, red-vectored people (and particularly children) can be praised for any reason or even without one. They blossom with praise and can never get enough — stopping the compliments forces them to fill the void by praising themselves. Bragging is a common sign that a red vector has not had its fill of praise.

The other side of the coin is that it kills red-vectored people when they have to praise others. After all, subconsciously (or consciously) they consider themselves the best and smartest, while complimenting someone else means acknowledging an equal and weakening their grip on the hierarchy in place. Only very mature and advanced red-vectored people who have gotten over their complexes and ambitions are able to sincerely admire others.

WORK

Red-vectored people stand out in whatever job they choose for their burning ambition, conceit, pride, and thirst for power. If they fall short of their goals, they sometimes torment the people around them with all kinds of schemes and changes they never find time to fully implement.

Besides roles in management and politics, they enjoy extreme sports and risk-based professions that offer the opportunity to show off their derring-do: working as combat engineers, life-guards, and the like. We could also add here the activities that have already been mentioned: water-related (swimmer, sailor, fisherman), fire-related (fire-fighter, pyrotechnician), and flight-related (fighter pilot, astronaut). Red-vectored people also make excellent scientists and inventors, pioneering various areas in science and technology. Additionally, they are capable of putting together impressive military careers as long as they have the other vectors (black and orange) needed for that particular occupation.

As soon as a red-vectored person gets a new idea lodged in

his head, he dives right in and forgets about everything else. And it does not matter what anyone else says — even if the mission seems impossible, he needs to be sure of that himself. On the other hand, to paraphrase Albert Einstein, discoveries are made by those who never knew they were impossible.

Schooling works the same way for red-vectored children: they study what interests them and let the rest slide, no matter how hard their parents and teachers push them. Quite often they collapse under the pressure from their teachers, quitting school to jump right into the adult life they have wanted practically since before they were born.

Certainly, the red vector can make people remarkable and even genius in practically any profession or area of their lives, as this vector is a catalyst capable of turbo-charging other vectors and making them all the more clearly defined.

If you ask a red-vectored adult about the work he has done in his lifetime, you will have a hard time believing the answer. Listing all the different employments he has had would take quite a while, with many of them pulled from entirely different and even contradicting areas.

Now imagine a person born with two strong vectors: brown and red. What would she look like?

That depends primarily on how both vectors are accepted. If they are both accepted and balanced, she could be very successful in widely varying areas of her life. She would be equally capable of beginning things (coming up with ideas) and finishing them, suited for both fast-paced and slower work, able to look at the big picture and focus in on the details, and a person of both the future and the past (ultimately, a person of the present!). The red/brown combination is therefore considered the most productive mix of two vectors.

Of course, not many people with that lucky combination reach their full potential. In fact, poor acceptance of their vectors leaves them in an unenviable position: they live, as it were, in two dimensions, thrown from side to side between two opposing vectors that cannot manifest themselves at the same time. Accustomed to a fast-paced, red-vectored life and unaware that their red vector is giving way to their brown vector, they start to worry when they suddenly notice their thought process and the speed at which they live dramatically slowing. Instead of leveraging the advantages that come with times like that to quietly wrap up everything they have previously started, they try whipping themselves into shape in order to hang on to that peak red-vector productivity. Ultimately and sadly, they burn out professionally, lose interest in work and life, and begin to suffer from psychological and somatic symptom disorders.

All it means when one vector lets another take over is that the first simply needs some time to relax before resuming its place on the front lines. Even our internal organs have their set peak times during the day, and none work at the same pace from morning until night. The same is true for vectors, which can go dormant for a few hours (that occurs differently for different people). With that in mind, avoid forcing yourself — instead, try to pay close attention to what your body is telling you and use what you have to work with at any given moment.

VECTOR MANAGEMENT

Many readers are probably wondering right now, "How do I turn the right vector on at the right time? How do I make sure my vectors help me instead of getting in the way? Sometimes, of course, you need to hurry right when your brown vector kicks in to slow you down... You need to clean up around the house, but you feel so lazy..."

There is only one tool that gives you control over your vectors, though that control is only indirect. Regardless, people who are equipped with it enjoy vectors that turn on right when they are needed, instead of the other way around. You are already familiar with that tool: *acceptance*. People who accept their natural vectors find that they automatically kick in just when they are most in demand. Need to do something physical? There goes your black vector. Need to understand something quickly? Here comes your red vector to the rescue. Have to finish something? That is a job for your brown vector. On the other hand, if your vectors are poorly or not at all accepted, they will pop their heads up at the worst possible moments to annoy you and make you unproductive.

There is no other way of managing vectors. You can certainly down a few cups of coffee to keep going a little longer (coffee works in our bodies as a substitute for uric acid, which is why it stimulates the red vector for some people), but the effect is brief and not overly physiological.

We can illustrate the balance with which this system works by looking at our stomach. When it is healthy, eating a bite of bread triggers the production of a special gastric juice designed to digest bread. On the other hand, eating a bite of meat triggers the production of an entirely different gastric juice designed to digest meat. Healthy stomachs work flawlessly; however, for a sick stomach, eating a bite of bread might trigger it to produce the gastric juice used to digest meat. But what meat is there to digest? Sadly, only the stomach itself, which is how gastritis and many other problems get started.

Vectors work the same way: acceptance lets them work like a healthy stomach.

OTHER CHARACTERISTICS

Balanced red-vectored people often find luck to be squarely on their side. Even in the most unlikely situations — ones where others usually lose — they win or at least break even. They also tend to be carefree with their money even as they tend to find themselves with plenty of it if their vector is completely accepted.

People like this hate lines and large-scale events, and cannot stand crowds unless they are at the front of them.

Red-vectored people do not have a particular affinity for food, though they prefer more salt than others and tend to drink more than they eat. The stronger their drink, the better, which is why expensive spirits make great gifts for them.

They speak energetically and quickly, often in such a hurry that they swallow the ends of their words ("you know what I mean"). While talking, they often exaggerate facts and figures: "I caught an enormous pike yesterday, must have been 45 pounds!" (...the fish was actually normal-sized), "I've been here for two hours waiting for you!" (...when you are a few minutes late), or "There's nothing in the fridge at all!" (...children often say this if they cannot find their yogurt or ketchup).

Red-vector handwriting can vary widely, though it is generally careless — marked by large spaces between lines that can run up or down, letters of different sizes, and frequent stains, strike-throughs, and inserts. Incidentally, using arrows to insert missing words is a common giveaway for the red vector. They also sometimes forget to finish words ("you know what I mean") and forego punctuation. To put it simply, you can tell if a text, even on the computer, has been written by a red-vectored author from a mile away, as it is strongly characteristic and easy to recognize.

Their behavior behind the wheel also reflects the main tendencies featured by the red vector: speed, freedom, and first place. Driving as fast as the engine will allow (who needs brakes?), a subconscious need to drive through their *favorite* color at traffic lights, and rushing right past cars parked nearby are only a few of the habits red-vectored people exhibit on the road. The passenger side window handle in their car is often torn off, while the dents in the floor on the same side make the passenger seat suitable for only the coolest of customers. Most important is getting into intersections *first* to make sure no one else can cut them off. All in all, their driving is symbolic of how red-vectored people approach their careers, business, talking with the opposite gender, and many other areas of their lives.

One more red-vector trait related to lifestyle and inattention to detail is a carelessness that starts at birth. It often looks like this type of person prefers living and working in utter chaos, with drawers and cabinets spilling out right into the middle of the room. However, regardless of the awful (creative) mess, red-vectored people know exactly where everything is.

They often forget to turn off the lights when they leave, walk away from running faucets and open doors, and hate clearing the table, making their bed, and cleaning their shoes. Training them to be orderly is nearly impossible (only if born with other vectors, for example brown or orange).

While brown-vectored people manage to pour identical amounts of tea into different cups when serving it (going back to their natural love of fairness), red-vectored people only get half a cup's worth into the actual cup. The rest spills onto the table.

The fact that a red-vectored person spent a long time in the tub does not mean that he is clean; he may have just been having a good time. Later that evening he might put his left sock under the bed and the right one on the table, completely confident that he will easily find both of them in the morning. If your brown vector makes you put them where they belong, you can be sure you are in for trouble.

APPEARANCE

Red-vectored people do not care about their appearance as long as they are wearing comfortable clothes. The freedom and independence they crave can pop up in little details of their clothing: an unbuttoned top button or unequally rolled-up sleeves for men or long red nails and bright red lipstick for women. Hairstyles are also quite free, with some locks sticking out in different directions or stacked asymmetrically. Holes and stains in their suits are the finishing touches they apply to their wardrobe: "and this one is...coffee!" Incidentally, a little hole in a woman's tights can be a strong turn-on for red-vectored men (the opposite is true of the brown vector). You might also have come across a red-vectored woman who only had time to put makeup on one eye.

Of course, everything in this description is strongly overstated, meaning that it is rare to find someone who stands out quite like this. Regardless, carelessness most often makes red-vectored people stick out in a crowd.

They also have typical gestures and poses that demonstrate their freedom, authority, and special territorial (or property) rights. For example, they sometimes sit with an arm draped over the next chair or their neighbor's shoulders. They even enjoy sleeping with their arms flung out so as to take up the entire bed.

HEALTH

Red-vectored people do not give much thought to their own health, caring only once they are already sick.

Given that their urogenital system is particularly sensitive, all kidney and bladder disorders as well as all diseases related to the male and female sexual organs can be traced back to the red vector. Of course, they only appear when the vector is not completely accepted and imbalanced (pressured, stifled, or simply unfulfilled), which is why, as strange as this might seem, *learning about* this vector's characteristics (by attending seminars or reading books) is sometimes enough for a dramatic improvement in the health of the patient. Our theory posits that diseases occur in organs (systems) where the person has increased sensitivity (a strong vector) but that do not receive enough stimulation (pleasure). If the red vector is realized in its mains areas (freedom, sexuality, and so on), there will be no reason for a sickness to occur in the Organism. *Consciousness* is the first step toward realizing a vector, and sometimes it is the only one needed.

Diseases suffered by the red vector also include the aforementioned alcoholism and drug addiction that are resorts for those who cannot develop personally or have even deeper problems. Certainly, venereal diseases can also be included on this list.

One last tendency is important to note when discussing red-vector health. If there is significant unacceptance (imbalance), many of the vector's features can be replaced by their opposites — a condition referred to as *red-vector neurosis*. Strong sexuality is replaced by impotence or frigidity; passion for water, heights, and darkness are replaced by fear of the same. People suffering from this condition see their thought process slow and their creativity vanish along with their charisma and ability to manage people.

ALGORITHM FOR RESOLVING NEUROSIS (APPLICABLE TO ALL VECTORS)

1. Be aware of which vector is suffering from neurosis (in other words, which is poorly accepted, pressured, or stifled). You can use the results of the test or go by your own gut feeling.

2. Where possible, think of a situation (for example, from your childhood) when that vector was strongly repressed. This

step is not essential, though it often proves highly beneficial.

3.   Look for any of your vector's needs that you *would like* to meet but currently are not (sometimes this means carefully rereading the appropriate chapter).

4.   Begin meeting that need little by little.

5.   A few days later note your vector's new needs that are appearing and go straight back to step four.

6.   A few weeks later sense that your vector has found a balance that is new to you, congratulating yourself on a victory won without a single casualty. You have now unlocked all the potential that vector offers (all its productive qualities), while you can also recognize that its unproductive qualities have all but disappeared.

Red-vectored people have one more problem complicating their lives: once they achieve a goal they have worked long and hard for and their long-awaited dream comes true, life becomes drab and boring. They no longer find pleasure in what they used to long for, even wondering what could possibly have once drawn them to it. That condition leads them to a depression that is difficult to come out of on their own (this may actually be why red-vectored people do not finish what they start, sensing as they do the future emptiness that awaits them). Instead, they sometimes turn to the short-term relief provided by alcohol or antidepressants.

There are two ways out of a situation like that. The first is to have the next goal or dream always ready and immediately start working toward it. The second is to start with unachievable goals. What do all the great physicists dream of? Inventing a perpetual-motion machine. Such an apparatus has never been created, though many great discoveries have been made along the way. Those scientists would probably not have been so productive had they not set their eyes on such a grand target.

LOVE AND SEX

While red-vectored people tend to stand out in many areas, their sexual potential is particularly strong. Reproduction is crucial to a successful future, and the alpha has a subconscious urge to personally take part in that process. Among all the vectors, the red vector enjoys the strongest, even hypersexual potential. If a red-vectored man tries to have sex with a woman, it does not mean that he is in love with her or thinks she is an easy catch; he is simply programmed by nature to have sex with all women at least once.

Red-vectored men in the throes of passion can be unusually generous, prepared as they are to overcome all obstacles and spend all the money they have on the women they desire. However, that does not keep them from asking the next morning, "Hey, what's your name?" Once turned on, they throw out promises right and left they have every intention of keeping when they give them. That does not at all guarantee that they will be kept, though, as red-vectored men answer to no one — they give when they want and take back when it no longer suits them.

As far as sex is concerned, these gentlemen are highly original, if short-lived. Women joke that they are like amusement parks: all the fun rides you could dream of, though none last longer than three minutes...

This area is similar to all the rest in that red-vectored people do their best to be as free as possible, meaning there is no sense asking them to be faithful. In fact, it is better to allow or even suggest that they take a lover on the side. Most often that means they will not take you up on your offer (and if they do, it will be just barely), partly due to their own insecurity complex: why test fate if everything is already permitted? For red-vectored people *consciousness* of their freedom is much more important than *acting on* that freedom.

Regardless of their strong sexual potential, red-vectored men are very vulnerable in this sphere of their lives — intimacy dials up their insecurity. If a woman impugns a brown-vectored man's masculinity in a moment of passion, he will spend three days going over that moment in his head and weighing the pros and cons before finally concluding that it is not true. If the same thing were said to a red-vectored man, he would immediately run and shoot himself or jump off a bridge.

The hypersexuality enjoyed by people like this begins early in childhood with a heightened interest in their own and others' intimate places. Red-vectored young adults also have a habit of regularly masturbating.

An old acquaintance once visited a vector training seminar I was running after having some problems raising her five-year-old son. The boy was giving her some real problems with his early sexual development. At the end of the lesson on the red vector she told me with some confusion, "Yes, I get it now... I get that why he needs to do all that... But he... sits there grunting like a grown man!!!"

So what can you do with this kind of child? The best thing to do is recognize that your child has that need and help him or her find a way to meet it respectably. Instead of simply telling them to stop, try saying something like, "You can, but..." Follow that up by laying out ground rules: only when they are alone, only when no one can hear or see them, only with clean hands, not at kindergarten or at school, and so on. Your child will be so surprised to be allowed to continue that he or she will happily stay within your limits.

Red-vectored boys and girls tend to mature quickly, both physically and psychologically. Their sexual lives begin sooner than most, and they also get pregnant sooner. In fact, young adults full of sexual desires and surrounded by limits and rules are at risk of proving their freedom dangerously by hitting the streets to develop a liking for alcohol and narcotics. That is why parents who are attentive and careful with regard to the sexuality of their children can both save them from going down the wrong road and make them the kind of outstanding, red-vectored people they want them to be.

Another interesting peculiarity of the red vector is a sexual predilection for elderly partners, something that in its full form is called *gerontophilia* (from the Greek *geron*, which means old, and *philie*, or love). This tendency might have deep evolutionary roots, as the alpha (the most sexually active male) has to be able to please all the females in the herd. He would have to start not with the best-looking (young and sexually attractive), but with the oldest (those whose biological clocks will soon run out).

We can continue looking at this topic by drawing on Little

Red Riding Hood, the well-known fairy tale.

A young, attractive girl sets off through a scary forest to bring cakes to her grandmother. In the forest she meets a lone wolf (remember that they are red-vectored) and, perhaps having heard how forest meetings with representatives of the red vector end, is very afraid. The hungry (!) wolf, learning that there is an old grandmother living nearby, leaves the young and beautiful girl in the forest with her cakes to head off in search of the grandmother (obviously an unusual step). Once he gets into the grandmother's home, he gets in bed with her and devours her (in psychology, that is a symbol of taking control — children who want to claim something stick it in their mouths). To use adult terminology, the wolf has the grandmother in her bed, after which he waits there and does the same to Little Red Riding Hood. Why the hungry (!) wolf leaves the young girl in the forest even after he learned where the grandmother lived is to this day a mystery to folklore enthusiasts. Not a single child or adult could explain the logic in the story.

This story symbolizes how red-vectored people find adult partners much more intriguing, only later turning to younger ones. This is true of both young men, who often prefer adult sexual partners, and hypersexual red-vectored girls who much prefer older, experienced men.

Red-vectored women are by their nature made for sex and childbirth. They get pregnant at the drop of a hat, doing so with such force and unpredictability that contraceptives are powerless. Childbirth itself usually happens easily and quickly, sometimes even being very pleasurable. On the other hand, they make poor parents, happily handing their children off to brown-vectored grandparents, sisters, or friends while they get back onto the rollercoaster that is red-vector life.

Incidentally, red-vectored women sometimes have a strong distaste for foreplay. If their men take too long getting through that step (buying flowers, talking, drinking tea, having coffee, or dancing), they may get fed up with it all and send them home. Imagine, there are women who do not care for anything that makes them wait for sex — after all, life is too fast-paced to get caught up in the preparation.

Red-vectored people love experimenting with sex, trying everything they can in search of something new and unusual. Often their fantasies get so carried away that inexperienced partners — and especially those without the red vector — get scared off. Living with a conservative partner like that as a red-vectored person, of course, is boring and dull.

On the other hand, life in a family with two strongly red-vectored people is anything but tedious. Instead, it is a continuous battle for leadership that ranges from basic everyday issues (who will make coffee today) to how to steer their lives together. Sex for those two red-vectored people, on the other hand, is incomparable in its passion, emotion, and depth of feeling. The marriage will probably not be long, as it is a brutal battle for superiority interrupted by unusual harmony in the bedroom that quickly burns them both out. "I can't live with you, and I can't live without you" is a common problem red-vectored people have in this situation.

We have spent this entire section talking about sex, but what about love? The red vector is probably the only one for which these two concepts are fused into one: "I love the one I want." And of course, "I always want the one I love."

If you are planning a wedding with a red-vectored person, do not forget that they are capable of changing their mind at the very last minute. It might seem strange, but that has nothing to do with you — they simply decided to take a different road...

Viktor Tolkachev enjoyed telling how to get a red-vectored man to marry you.

"First you take a walk in the general area, but not on the same street as the church. Start with the next one over to let him get used to it. Then gradually try walking by the church without acknowledging it in any way. At some point your red-vectored man, who sometimes has crazy ideas, will turn and ask you out of the blue, 'Want to go get hitched?' But be careful! What should your response be? 'Are you crazy? Are you feeling all right?!" That is a trap for your red-vectored man that will have him dragging you into the church a couple weeks later."

Is it possible to have a long-lasting relationship with a person like this? Of course it is. There are even red-vectored people who go many years without cheating on their partners, though only if those partners are highly creative (usually in the bedroom) and always ready for surprises.

CONVERSATION AND MOTIVATION

Red-vectored people are easy to talk to if you bear in mind the peculiarities of their vector. If you need something from them, do not forget that they need to be the initiators instead of you. That holds true for both children and young adults.

However, if you are not able to wait for them to take the first step, remember this magic phrase: "You're our only hope!" It works beautifully when said with complete sincerity, letting you sit back and watch them move mountains for you.

There is no other way to manipulate the red vector, as it cannot be bought and is very difficult to convince. Even if red-vectored people do change their minds, they do so because they decided to instead of being convinced. I hope you will not try to point out your own role in the change of heart.

There is only one effective way to motivate red-vectored people: play to their insecurity. Expressing doubt about their abilities (publically, in particular) makes it extraordinarily hard for them not to prove that they actually are completely capable. That type of scenario can be especially dangerous for red-vectored teenagers, for whom the desire to assert their status in the group can push them to make tragic mistakes.

In contrast with the brown vector, the red vector needs to have grandiose goals. Children who cannot picture a great future for themselves have no reason to study, which is why they are perfectly fine looking past school to the days when they will be president of the Academy of Sciences (their habit of not finishing things will keep them from actually becoming president, though they could very well become vice president).

A group with two strongly red-vectored people will see them wage a full-fledged battle for control that generally has one of two outcomes: either the system as a whole splits into two subsets led respectively by the two leaders, or the more red-vectored of the two crowds out the competition.

WRAPPING UP: BRINGING THE RED VECTOR HOME

We can sum up the contents of this chapter by saying that the red vector is exemplified in life across six main areas:

1. Adrenaline — extreme activities, including professions, hobbies, and habits

2. Speed — in thought, action, and decision

3. Sex — strong sexual potential (frequency and variety)

4. Power — ability and desire to manage people, events, and Life itself

   — from everyone and everything

6. Self-realization — numerous and widely varying personal talents and abilities

Any of these six areas can be repressed in childhood by parents or other significant adults. As you already know, that repression leads to poor acceptance and ultimately red-vector neurosis. It is important to remember that the red vector is more easily repressed than many others, while red-vectored people (especially children) fall more easily into neurosis.

I would like to conclude this chapter with the symbol of fire we used to describe the red vector. I once heard this phrase, and, though I do not remember where I heard it, it has stayed with me all these years as the best characterization of the red vector I know:

"A red-vectored person is a candle with two wicks burning at

the same time, making its flame both brighter and shorter-lived."

FILMS TO WATCH (WITH RED-VECTORED CHARACTERS)

- Mr. & Mrs. Smith, directed by Doug Liman, USA, 2005 (John and Jane Smith, played by Brad Pitt and Angelina Jolie)

- One Flew Over the Cuckoo's Nest, directed by Milos Forman, USA, 1975 (McMurphy, played by Jack Nicholson)

- Run Lola Run, directed by Tom Tykwer, Germany, 1998 (Lola, played by Franka Potente)

- Back to the Future, directed by Robert Zemeckis, USA, 1985 (Dr. Emmett Brown, played by Christopher Lloyd)

- Vicky Cristina Barcelona, directed by Woody Allen, Spain and USA, 2008 (Juan Antonio, played by Javier Bardem)

Visit my site www.psy8.net to enjoy the Vector Test, the Vector Gallery (pictures, movies and citations of all eight vectors), the article about the compatibility of vectors, answers to readers' questions, and more.

CHAPTER 4. THE BLACK VECTOR — NAVEL

In this chapter we will discuss the most unusual orifice our body has to offer, and one that is even difficult to call an orifice in the first place: the navel. But if a person's character is formed in their childhood as influenced by their sensitive orifices, how does a person whose main orifice is their navel build their character? It turns out that this is the only vector whose character is largely formed in the womb, a circumstance that leaves a life-long imprint — after all, existence in the womb is much different from what comes after birth...

LACTIC ACID

Have you ever done tough, physical work? How did you feel afterwards? I think many would say they feel tired and beat-up, how their muscles hurt, and how they just want to lay there doing nothing.

Those feelings in our body come from lactic acid, a substance produced in our muscles. Doing just a little work only produces a corresponding amount of lactic acid that is broken down in the liver and goes unnoticed. On the other hand, heavy or extensive exertion triggers the production of excessive lactic acid, affecting the pain receptors in our muscles to give us that feeling we know so well. Lactic acid also spreads throughout our organism and acts on the "displeasure centers" in the brain, explaining the broad spectrum of emotional reactions to physical exertion.

But that does not happen to everyone!

Some people are genetically blessed with a surprising ability: for them lactic acid affects their "pleasure centers." Our system relegates them to the black vector, one Viktor Tolkachev called the "muscular" or "umbilical" vector.

You can take the Vector Test on my site www.psy8.net

That unusual reaction to lactic acid explains the black vector's primary peculiarity: heavy, monotonous physical labor brings it bodily pleasure. There are even jokes about this kind of person: when you tell them to cut rails for railroad tracks, you have to tell them to do it crosswise instead of lengthwise. Their love of hard labor would have them cutting the long way, while the bridges they build would at least run diagonally to the river in an attempt to make the job last longer. And if you told them to build a wall without telling them how long to build it, they would keep going until the end looped all the way back around to meet the beginning. Of course, these old jokes are heavy on the exaggeration, though life itself is sometimes even stranger than fiction.

One winter I witnessed a fascinating scenario that illustrates what makes the black vector different. A snow-removal machine was clearing a snowy road. The driver was dead serious, sitting with his hands tightly clamped onto a steering wheel that was clearly bouncing around on the patches of ice on the road. There was quite a bit of snow, and the truck was handling it well, though...

You are doubtless familiar with how there is usually a dump truck behind snow removers to collect the snow they toss back. Behind this one, however, an identical machine with an equally serious driver was clearing the snow the first was simply shooting back onto the road. They were working together so well that it was a pleasure to watch. And then behind the second truck...

There was nothing behind the second truck, and the snow it cleared dropped right back onto the road. The whole situation was so captivating that I walked along beside them for a little while. I thought the dump truck might have run off to unload before returning to take its place in the caravan, but I was wrong: having reached an intersection, the two drivers got out, quietly had a smoke next to their machines, got back in, and continued on. I could tell from their faces that they saw nothing unreasonable in what they were doing.

This situation is reminiscent of an old joke about three workers who were supposed to plant a tree: the first dug the hole and the third filled it in, while the second (the one with the tree) called in sick.

How do we explain scenes like that? Simply: if work itself is brings happiness, the *point of the activity* is relegated to second place. For this kind of person, doing the work and enjoying the strained muscles and blood coursing through veins is most important. They live more through their bodies (muscles) than with their heads or sensory organs. And they will still do the work even if they know there is no grander meaning, simply for the sake of the bodily pleasure they derive from it. This is comparable to brown-vector behavior, where there is a compulsion to finish even jobs that are no longer needed.

But hold on! Do not think for a second that black-vectored people are stupid or crazy. They just have their peculiarities that need understanding and consideration just like any other vector. Brown-vectored people, for example, have just as much difficulty in stressful situations as black-vectored ones, while red-vectored brains shut off completely the moment they see a cute face (hands, legs) belonging to the opposite gender. Every vector has its own weaknesses.

WORK, BABY, WORK

Black-vectored people love work so much that they often unknowingly steal it from others. They are also bad at explaining to other people what to do, so they strongly prefer just doing it themselves.

We had an arts and crafts teacher like this at school. He would tell the class, "Okay, kids, today we're making paper airplanes. You take a piece of paper, fold it one-two-three, and done. Got it?" One boy answered, "No, not really..." "Here, give it to me. Watch: one-two-three, and done. Okay?" Another answered, "I don't think so..." "Give it to me... Watch..." And a third boy said the same. The teacher made seven paper airplanes before stopping for a moment and asking, "Do you think I'm an idiot?"

People for whom the black vector is predominant are drawn to physical labor. If their vector is simply an afterthought in a combination of other, stronger vectors, they may be workaholics — just not on the physical side of things. For example, there are botanists who spend weeks hard at work staring into their microscopes with just short breaks for food and sleep. They do not look black-vectored, but many of their psychological qualities speak directly to the fact that they do have that vector.

Black-vectored people spend the majority of their time wrapped up in their work, with much of their conversation at home, on vacation, and even at the workplace itself also occupied by the same topic. Many are simply incapable of relaxing, feeling ill at ease on the weekends and uncomfortable on vacation — all they want to do is head back to the work they know and love. "The best vacation is a new job," they would say, having a hard time imagining what it would be like to lay on the couch or on a beach. In fact, the only time black-vectored people do so is when they are in neurosis.

Black-vectored people attack their work with such zeal that you need to thoroughly discuss boundaries when giving them an assignment. Their love of work often leads them to pick the most complicated solution available — "shortcut-free zone" could hang above their desks. Occasionally they throw up obstacles for themselves only to pour all their energy into beating them, which may be why some refer to black-vectored people as busy forcing square pegs into round holes.

Children with strong black vectors are easy to spot in a sandbox. While their friends are building houses and garages, they take their bucket, fill it with sand, and — pow! — make their castle only to knock it over. Again they take their bucket, fill it with sand, and — pow! — first a castle, then knock it down. Alternatively, they may not be ready to go home until the entire sandbox is full of castles.

A uniform lack of variety is normal for the black vector, as both children and adults love rinsing and repeating the same activities and experiences. Black-vectored children can happily watch the same cartoon or listen to the same fairy tale every day for several months, as their routine affords them a sense of comfort and peace missing in everyday life.

MORE POWER TO THE MUSCLES

Black-vectored people, who prefer working with their hands, do their best not to overload their minds, as the former is much more pleasant to exert than the latter. There are many explanations for that, though I will offer only one I do not claim to necessarily be true or complete.

In order to work hard, our muscles need oxygen and energy that is delivered via the blood. However, there is only so much blood in the body, and when it is working overtime to keep up with our muscles (we generally work standing up) it needs to come from somewhere else... Yes, it has been posited that black-vectored people have poor circulation in their heads as compared to their muscles. That may be why they are uncomfortable with work that requires mental exertion.

Their thought process differs from that of other vectors in that it is practical instead of abstract. They also have an excellent, motor-based intellect where it is almost as if they think with their hands. Black-vectored people make very good craftsmen, and their handiwork makes it even more difficult to call them stupid or unintelligent. It is just that they are not good at generating new ideas or making important decisions; they execute wonderfully and to a degree that leaves many other vectors in the dust.

Incidentally, they are experts when it comes to their favorite job or sport.

Ancient times were great for black-vectored people, who happily went off to achieve their potential and work as craftsmen or farmers. Then the situation changed, with everyone required to get an education: "Sit there, boy, and study — burn the midnight oil!" However, they prefer moving and working with their hands to sitting in one place. Spending 45 minutes behind a desk is torture, as evidenced by their fidgeting and kicking. "Stop squirming! Sit still!" they hear from their teachers. And what can they do besides sit there waiting to run around during recess? The break finally arrives, but as soon as they take their first step they hear, "No running!" "Well," they think, "at least I can jump." But as soon as they get ready to take off they hear, "No jumping!" And so obedient black-vectored children spend their entire recess without moving around at all. Their heads, after all, have an unusual circulation system, and they end up getting worse and worse from all the standing and sitting. They come back to the next lesson "stupid and even stupider."

With black-vectored children it is crucial to mix mental and physical exertion. It has long been recognized that they think more clearly after PE lessons, in the morning (right after they get to school), and after long recesses (during which they have a chance to run and jump around). Robbing them of active movement leads to all that physical energy building up until it explodes at the most inopportune moment: they leave school, pick up a stone, and hurl it through a window. Avoid tormenting black-vectored children with too much education: once they have learned how to read, do math, and write, let them go work or play sports. Later they can come back to their schooling if they so desire, as forcing it on them just makes them hate it all the more.

It is important to remember that things come more easily to black-vectored people when put to them in a way they are used to. Many drill sergeants in the army are like this: you know how the black-vectored ones train their cadets? If they give a rule that is then retold using the student's own words, it is wrong. If the words are even the same but in a different order, it is still wrong. The only right way is "like I told you." The issue at stake is not authority, and the sergeant is not making fun of the cadets; instead, he is convinced that the initial idea can only be conveyed by repeating a set phrase.

Think about this: would a black-vectored child think more clearly if she were taught to stand on her head? It turns out that she would! It is no accident that many eastern forms of gymnastics employ headstands for children. The vector system has already demonstrated this to be a fact: while the child's black vector does not weaken, improved cranial circulation boosts cognition.

Black-vectored people think with their hands, but also with their entire bodies. They have a close connection to their bodies (if, of course, their vector is accepted) that is the envy of other vectors, as that contact offers both physical and spiritual health.

As well, black-vectored people have a particular affinity and even love for soil that begins in childhood — they have a great time working with the ground and digging in gardens. They feel close to nature (they love going to sleep and getting up with the sun), have a connection with the earth, and have a built-in compass. Their affinity for the world around them and their motor-based intellect keeps them from ever getting lost in the forest, even if they have no orienteering training whatsoever. If they do get lost, all they have to do is follow their gut instinct and watch it take them back to where they are supposed to be.

CREATOR OR DESTROYER?

If this vector is fully accepted and realized, there is no one more physically healthy than black-vectored people. Even beyond that, they are also psychologically healthy, being stable, reliable, and loyal. They are the kind of people who never let you down.

Look around you — everything you see was made by black-vectored hands or machines that were also made (but not invented!) by them. Everything you eat was planted, grown, and harvested by black-vectored people manually or by machine.

Black-vectored people are Earth's Creators and the main manufacturers of material things. They are protectors and hunters, builders and craftsmen. The majority of our society's most important functions are fulfilled by this vector.

However, if the black vector is not accepted or realized (if it is repressed or stifled), other navel-related urges appear. Those urges are what turn Earth's main Creators into its primary Destroyers, a process you know well.

When a baby is growing in the womb, its muscular system begins to function much sooner than its eyes, ears, nose, and other sensory organs. While green-vectored (eyes), blue-vectored (ears), and violet-vectored (nose) children are not yet able to satisfy their significant zones, black-vectored (navel and muscles) children even in the womb can get pleasure from their own movements. They kick and punch regularly beginning even at the early stages of pregnancy in an attempt to maximize their enjoyment, meaning that the prenatal life of black-vectored children is much more experience-packed than those of other-vectored children. Of course, life in the womb for all children (regardless of their vectors) is comfortable, cozy, nourishing, warm, quiet, and safe if the mother leads a healthy life. The enjoyment received by black-vectored children in the womb, however, cannot be compared with the other vectors, since **they are the only ones** who can benefit from additional pleasure from their significant zone. As a result, black-vectored babies often hold on to that happy world they treasure so deeply as long as they possibly can.

What happens when the child is born? It is instantly bereft of the happy place it was used to, which is why birth is always such a stressful moment. For black-vectored babies, however, that stress is exaggerated to the same degree its life "on the inside" was especially comfortable. A subconscious complex pulling them back toward the womb appears at birth, something exhibited in attempts to create an environment reminiscent of life back inside the mother: peace, stability, nourishment, protection, and no need to make decisions. In adulthood that desire appears as a particular way of nesting at home and at work as well as in the way personal lives are organized.

There is one more thing that is even more important. If life in the mother (in the womb) was wonderful, and birth introduces something entirely different, then "not-life" is better than life... And if we are living now, then "not-life" is death. That is why black-vectored people have a deep, subconscious complex that is destructive or necrophilial[6]. If the black vector is realized and satisfied, this complex remains in the subconscious without showing its head much in everyday life. However, if the black vector is not channeled in a peaceful direction (physical labor, sports, working the earth, and so on), destructive tendencies start to appear. In the extreme, the subconscious goal of a person like this is to destroy and annihilate everything around them. Even suicide takes on a wider focus: not simply "I'll kill myself," but "I will blow up/crash a plane full of people"...

But what is war from the point of view of a black-vector destroyer? It is a way of expressing one's self. However, war ends sooner or later, and the destructive habits unleashed stay and reenter peaceful society... Data shows that more American soldiers committed suicide after the Vietnam War than were killed during the war itself, as they turned the destruction on themselves. It takes a horde of psychologists to help returning warriors assimilate back into life on the home front.

You might be wondering about World War II, after which people went back to their peaceful lives without any of that sort of destruction. Well, in the 1940s and 1950s there was much to build and create, keeping black-vectored people and their main calling in high demand. Today soldiers coming back from hot spots are largely unneeded, making it hard for them to transition back into the black vector's creative frame of mind.

Incidentally, that same black-vectored child in the sandbox will happily knock over both their own and the other children's

---

[6] Viktor Tolkachev referred to this complex as necrophilial given the basic urge toward not only destruction, but literal and figurative death.

sand castles. Well, at least then it is only sand.

A VIEW TOWARD THE INSIDE

Black-vectored people are intrigued by their own insides and that of others, both literally and figuratively. In its positive iteration (when the vector is accepted), this interest leads to eastern philosophy and religion, meditation, and deep study of the internal world. Negatively (when the vector is in neurosis), this interest turns to a primitive question: "What do his insides look like?" Repressed black-vectored people make excellent Jack the Rippers.

Moved by this interest, black-vectored children enjoy tearing toys (soft, hard, mechanical, and all the rest) into pieces. Red-vectored children are also interested to see what is inside their toys (this is especially true of mechanical ones), pulling them apart, check them out, and putting them back together (the toy often goes back to working normally, even though a few pieces are somehow left over). Black-vectored children, on the other hand, could not care less about putting their toys back together, leaving them shredded after they get their glimpse of the insides and lose interest.

Avoid suppressing this vector in childhood by helping your child find things that can safely be taken apart. If you do harshly restrain this behavior, the internal urge will still rear its head at some point (when there are no parents around to stop it) and the subject will be something more valuable or even an animal.

In adulthood it is dangerous not to understand one's own destructive and necrophilial complex. Being conscious of that urge for death means it can be channeled by working in a morgue, cemetery, or slaughterhouse. If that understanding and acceptance is missing, those tendencies go uncontrolled, appearing at the worst possible moment.

While brown-vectored sadists attack their victim waiting for tears and never killing them, black-vectored necrophiliacs thirst for death. Their victims' tears only hasten the process...

CHARACTER AND HABITS

Black-vectored people are introverts and phlegmatics, marked by their reliability, modesty, perseverance, and self-control. They are trusting in how they relate to people, with a firm devotion those around them sometimes exploit. Occasionally their submission morphs into dependence on the authority figures around them: a crowd of these obedient "soldiers" is easy to manage, especially considering that black-vectored people easily replace their own interests with those of the group.

They are also characterized by a collective mentality that has them only rarely talking about themselves as a singular entity: instead of "I," they often use "we" to include those around them. That is partly because of their inability to take responsibility and partly due to evolutionary inclinations, as there were no "black" functions in ancient times that could be handled alone (hunting for food, protecting against enemies, building, and so on). That may be why black-vectored people prefer not to make decisions. As you recall, brown-vectored people also have trouble making choices, though after agonizing for a while they do ultimately make a final decision. They would otherwise, after all, not have the satisfaction of getting the job done. For black-vectored people the situation is completely different. Telling them to make a decision for themselves puts them in a difficult situation — they much prefer to trust nearby authority figures rather than forge their own way if at all possible. The role of authority figure could be played, for example, by their wife, friend, boss, or trainer.

Nature may have gifted the black vector with an unusual character trait to make up for these qualities: unusual willpower that helps get them through tough situations and keep moving toward their set goal (this is a scarce quality among red-vectored people who, regardless of their passionate fieriness, burn out quickly when met with obstacles). This black-vector willpower has made it possible to throw up unique structures in many countries that might seem impossible (the Egyptian pyramids and the Great Wall of China are two examples). The same quality has driven some to save hundreds of lives by throwing themselves in front of enemy machine guns.

Black-vectored people are very conservative, having once built a picture of something that should never change. "There's no sacrificing principles" is their most fundamental motto. Brown-vectored people are also given to set views, though they can be persuaded to change their minds over time and with undeniable proof. It is almost impossible to get black-vectored people to change their minds.

People like this have a hard time getting through crises in their lives. Losing their job or a close friend, something that wreaks havoc on the relationships they are used to, puts them in a stupor during which they sit for hours or days wondering how to go on living. Knowing how they respond to similar events, black-vectored people are watchful against (and even respond aggressively toward) any hint of change in their lives. They are the opponents of change at home and in the workplace, joining forces with the retrograde[7] brown vector.

Black-vectored people obey the law, though which law they obey is a separate issue: sometimes they fall in line with the constitution, and other times they follow other principles. They often turn to religion, even those who do the "blackest" work there is.

A man comes to church and prays, "God, forgive me for killing one man yesterday and another the day before. Forgive me also for tomorrow's job, as I will not have time to come." And through it all completely serious...

Their emotional background is very stable, without sharp ups or downs, and it is hard to make them very angry. However, if you do, watch out. Black-vectored people are like train cars loaded with iron: they are hard to get moving, but once rolling they flatten everything in their path.

Black-vectored people have no idea how to handle situations requiring quick reactions, preferring to do the monotonous work they love at a slow pace. The ideal job for them is running a production line.

They avoid responsibility, widely ranging contacts, and too much information, all of which serves only to complicate and destabilize their lives (the less you know, the better you sleep).

---

[7] Retrograde (from the Latin retrogrades, meaning to go backward), or being opposed to progress, a person constantly looking backward.

Black-vectored people can drink large amounts of alcohol without getting drunk or becoming alcoholics. Having downed a bottle of vodka, they can drive off and quietly get home with eyes that are just about closed — their instinct takes over so long as the road is familiar and there are no detour signs.

Clothing, food, and living arrangements for black-vectored people are modest and unassuming. They prefer reliable, functional things: everything has its own use, so do not even try giving them ornamental knick-knacks.

They generally have no use for the caprices of fashion, wearing practical and durable clothing that does not infringe on their movement (many prefer track suits).

Black-vectored people sleep soundly, going straight into a deep sleep as soon as the flow of external information ceases. Their affinity for nature leads them to prefer a physiological lifestyle, going to sleep and getting up earlier.

They eat quite a bit of food that never varies, doing so both when they are hungry and when there just happens to be food nearby. They are like phones with worn-out batteries: if there is an outlet nearby, they need to be charging.

A social event is in full swing and features a buffet loaded with food. A man with a stereotypical black-vector build is standing by one of the tables and stuffing sandwich after sandwich into his mouth, while off in the corner stands a skinny, blue-vectored programmer eating nothing. The black-vectored man gestures over to him, "Why aren't you eating anything? Look how much there is! Dig in!". The other fellow, anxious to avoid a one-sided discussion, picks up a small sandwich and nibbles at it. The black-vectored man is less than satisfied: "You call that eating?!" "Well, you know... I just eat when I'm hungry..." "What are we, animals?!"

Black-vectored people think better while moving: it is no accident that black-vectored children move instinctively — walking around or gesturing with their hands — the whole time they are learning poems or writing on a blackboard. Their muscle memory may even help with memorizing and regurgitating abstract ideas.

However, there are some things black-vectored people have a hard time with even while moving: they find it incredibly difficult to focus on multiple things at once or jump back and forth from one to another. On the other hand, they are extraordinarily good at focusing on one thing, a quality that can be applied to deep meditation and other widely varying areas in their lives.

BACK TO THE WOMB

One of the most important aspects of life in the mother's womb is the cramped quarters, or, more accurately, the feeling of having another body always next to you. Black-vectored people do their best to recreate that sensation in their own lives: they love being in crowds, living and working in tight spaces, playing team sports, participating in huge events, and taking public transportation during rush hour.

While brown-vectored people begin construction of their vacation home with the bathroom and red-vectored people start with the pool, black-vectored people first install a fence! And no little picket fence either — they put in a three-meter reinforced concrete wall (a tank would have a hard time getting through!). Strongly black-vectored people generally build a durable home behind that wall with small (often round) windows that look like gun loopholes. It is only in that kind of house and behind *that* kind of wall *that* they feel safe, as if they were back in the womb.

Do you think babies in the womb see light or colors? Sadly, they live in pitch darkness, though our eyes are designed such that even in completely darkness we can "see" something like a dark red color. That is why black-vectored people have two favorite colors: black, of course, and that same dark red. Their favorite shape is the rectangle (or brick).

An important quality for black-vectored people is the love they have for their mothers. Although they do not generally turn into "mommy's babies," their special connection and deep reverence for their mothers last from birth until death. That connection may be due to the peculiarities of the vector's prenatal life. One way or another, mom's opinion is very important and authoritative to them, and the principles they get from her stick with them the rest of their lives.

WORK AND CAREERS

As you already know, black-vectored people are our society's primary creators of material goods. This vector, in fact, is the keystone of any system.

Black-vectored people happily spend many years doing the same job, valuing as they do stability, a friendly environment, honesty, and simple communication. The black vector is the most loyal of all the vectors, making them dedicated to and prepared to sacrifice much for their companies.

They do not usually focus too much on the career ladder, though being recognized as a critical cog in the machine is important to them. Note that this is their most significant motivational factor at the workplace.

Employees like this are valued for their productivity, endurance, healthiness, ability to get along with everyone, and habit of never getting tired. "You have to" is a magic phrase for them, and one that, if spoken by an authority figure, is never questioned. They simply get the job done.

It is difficult for black-vectored people to learn new professions (books and instruction manuals are better saved for brown-vectored people), with apprenticeships the best option for them (just as it was with craftsmen and farmers way back when).

Of course, sports that require strength and endurance are perfect for the black vector. However, careers in sports end sooner or later and there are only so many coaching jobs, so black-vectored people are left with a tricky question when their careers ultimately come to an end: what should they do next? Sometimes their talents find application in the criminal world, where physical (and emotional) strength is always in demand.

Their physical and psychological qualities make black-vectored people excellent soldiers, though, in contrast to the red vector, a military career does not interest them. The army is something like the womb for the black vector: there is stability, the necessary minimal comforts (food and drink), the feeling of a shoulder next to one's own, and no need to make decisions or choices. You just eat, drink, train, and do what you are told.

Black-vectored people also love animals, and especially the

big ones, which is why they often become veterinarians (if they have the other necessary vectors as well, of course). Remember how I talked about another vector that enjoys the process of communicating with horses itself when talking about the brown vector's love of riding? That, of course, is the black vector, with people who do not simply ride horses; they dream of having their own to take care of and look after. A love of horses is highly characteristic of the black vector.

Ultimately, black-vectored people prefer professions related to: physical labor (worker, builder, athlete), the earth and nature (farmer, veterinarian), working with their hands (craftsman, production line worker), death (worker at the morgue, a cemetery, or a slaughterhouse), and the military (enlisted soldier).

LOVE AND SEX

Black-vectored people enjoy a sexual potential that is higher than average (third among the vectors), while they may not have much of a sexual appetite. They happily exchange physical labor for sex.

"The greatest feeling you can get in a gym, or the most satisfying feeling you can get in a gym, is the pump. Let's say you train your biceps — blood is rushing into your muscles, and that's what we call the pump. Your muscles get a really tight feeling, like your skin is going to explode any minute. You know, it's really tight; it's like somebody blowing air into your muscles. It just blows up and you feel different, it feels fantastic. It's as satisfying to me as coming is, you know, as having sex with a woman and coming. So can you believe how much I am in heaven? I am like getting the feeling of

coming in the gym, I'm getting the feeling of coming at home, I'm getting the feeling of coming backstage when I pump up, when I pose out in front of 5,000 viewers, I get the same feeling. So I am coming day and night! I mean, that's terrific, right? So, you know, I'm in heaven!"

— Arnold Schwarzenegger in Pumping Iron, a documentary released in 1977

Black-vectored men are indefatigable in the bedroom, if unvaried. While red-vectored men are like an amusement park with a variety of exciting carousels that all last just three minutes, black-vectored men are like a simple carousel in an old park spinning in one direction and at one speed for a long time. But can you imagine a man with both the red and black vectors? He would be a sex machine!

Black-vectored people are reliable, faithful partners who are also good family men and women. A marriage between two black-vectored people is strong and balanced, with both of them working, exercising, or digging in the garden together.

Black-vectored men choose wives who look like their mothers. Remember, however, that the picture is more in line with their gut instinct, and so there may not be a physical similarity between the two.

HEALTH

As you are already aware, the black vector is the healthiest of the eight. Black-vectored people only rarely visit the doctor, though work (or some other kind of physical exertion) is the best medicine for the few times they do get sick.

Regardless of their strong constitution, however, black-vectored people often suffer from accidental and self-inflicted injuries like walking into a pole on their way down the street. They might also open their car door right into their eye — the problem is that they think they are as big and strong as an icebreaker. As they walk or drive, they have the feeling that the things in their path should make way for them, which sometimes does happen (though not always, as some things are immobile). That is how they get stuck trying to drive between two trees, for instance.

More serious health problems arise when black-vectored people cannot realize their potential at work or by some other form of physical exertion, while their conscience or upbringing does not allow them to tear down the world around them. In that case the black-vector organism may start destroying itself, as there are more than enough diseases to make that happen: tumors, cardiovascular problems, and much more, with age not mattering in the least.

APPEARANCE AND OTHER FEATURES

Black-vectored people are built fairly large and are more often than not muscular, though there are some exceptions (especially when the vector is not accepted). Their figures ooze strength and stability, while their movements are slow and exaggerated. There is practically no such thing as small movements, the lack of which sometimes seems somewhat constrained or laborious. Black-vector legs are set widely, take long steps, and sometimes even break into a bear-like lumbering waddle.

Black-vectored people enjoy their physical endowments by playing with their muscles and popping their joints, engendering responses from those around them that range from fear to admiration. They love shaking hands so strongly that the weaker party cowers a little with a grimace on their face, though they do not do so out of aggression — they are just letting everybody know who is strongest.

An important feature of the black vector is a heavy-set face that includes all of a large nose, enormous eyes, and a wide mouth. Their face shows few emotions and is minimally expressive, something that occasionally gets them referred to as "stony-faced" (think here of any security guard you have ever met). Their laughter is hollow and a little shy, with ghost movies using the sound from off-screen to scare viewers.

Black-vectored people prefer to buzz their hair or shave it altogether, and black-vectored men bald early thanks to their physiology.

The classic black-vectored woman wears makeup only rarely and has heavy facial features, a muscular build, and short hair. The term "weaker sex" sounds comic when applied to them, as many can easily handle any man.

CONVERSATION

Typical black-vectored people speak in a boring monotone. For them conversation is less about communication (their own body is enough for them) and more about exchanging information:

"Pass the salt." "Here you go." And there the conversation finishes...

They do not have an extensive vocabulary and often have a hard time finding the right words to say. On the other hand, they use quite a few interjections ("Wow! Unbelievable! That's crazy! Look at that! There you go! Holy moly!") and throw-away words ("Well, so, it's like, um, you know, basically"). Some black-vectored people swear profusely, though, in contrast to yellow-vectored people, they always use the same ones without emotion and only to fill in the pauses between words: "We... geez... yesterday... geez... were... oh, geez... here..." If you took out all the "geezes," what would you get? "Uhh...uhh..." Black-vectored people often make fun of themselves: "I don't use swear words to curse; I use them to talk."

They also have a hard time understanding implications, remaining unaware of double and hidden meanings in both speech and written language. With that in mind, if you enjoy that type of thing, something not many people understand, be careful around black-vectored people. They may take you quite literally.

The same is true of humor: if brown-vectored people have a hard time getting the joke, black-vectored people miss it altogether. They might even react to the joke in a very simple way: muscularly. That makes it better to be careful when joking around them, as you might get a shot to the eye before you have a chance to explain what you actually meant.

Body contact during conversation is important to black-vectored people: if you want them to remember what you are about to say, touch their hands. They themselves enjoy touching the people they are talking with, though that may turn into continually plucking at your sleeve or button.

Black-vectored people also prefer to converse from a very short distance, coming up so close to the person they are talking with that they violate their personal space without ever meaning to do so. Keeping in mind that blue- and green-vectored people like talking from a distance, you can imagine a conversation between a black-vectored person and one of them: one takes a step forward and the other shuffles backward, both movements happening subconsciously. They continue that little dance until the blue/green-vectored person leaves the room entirely.

BLACK-VECTOR NEUROSIS

If the black vector in ancient times was one of the most well-regarded in society (folk tales are often rooted in this time period), today many of its qualities, especially in children, are no longer welcome. That is why some black-vectored people grow up in an atmosphere hostile to what makes them different. As a result, they do not accept the vector in themselves, leading to the development of unproductive qualities and, in the extreme, black-vector neurosis: weakness, a weak will, and an aversion to physical exertion. A person like that no longer looks typically black-vectored, becoming instead slender and erratic.

This change in mindset has been especially hard on women: masculine qualities (read: the black vector) are belittled in our culture beginning at an early age. "You're a girl," they hear, "so you should flutter like a butterfly! Look at you knocking over tables..." That is why many women have an unaccepted black vector and all that entails.

Once a girl visited one of my training seminars. No matter how you looked at her, she was perfection: unusually beautiful, smart, educated, and well-off (house, career, luxury car, boyfriend, love). In short, everything was great.

At one lesson she came up to me, supposedly to ask about her girlfriend. She mentioned a few character traits and behaviors, finishing by asking, "And what vector is that?"

It did not take me long to answer: "The black vector, of course." The answer was so simple and obvious to me that her reaction came as a complete surprise.

The girl froze for a couple seconds (I had never seen her that confused), after which her face flushed and she angrily asked me, "You're saying I'm the most stupid???!!!"

The black vector needs to be accepted even if it is neither strong nor dominant. If that does not happen, normally energetic and sharp-witted people can from time to time fall into an unexpected stupor that surprises everyone around them as well as themselves. That is just the black vector making an appearance: without being fully realized in everyday life it pops its head up at the worst possible moment.

There are quite a few ways to accept the black vector: exercise, any kind of physical activity, working the soil (in the garden, for example), and visiting places that unabashedly welcome black-vector energy — sports games, protests, demonstrations, and other large-scale events.

If people have a black vector with excessively high potential but without the opportunity to let it play out in everyday life (because of particular health concerns or an unusual upbringing), its potential can turn destructive. And if the black vector is coupled with the red vector, which emphasizes other vectors, that destructiveness can take on huge proportions. We will return to that topic when we talk about the violet vector.

A BLACK-VECTOR KINGDOM

Let's try our hand building a black-vector kingdom. Imagine that there are millions of us and that we are almost all black-vectored. We will need government emblems (a flag, a national anthem, and some kind of holy symbol), a primary activity, and so forth. The flag is simple enough: it will just be black (with a skull and crossbones) or dark red. The holy symbol is a bit more complicated, as it needs to be important, deep, and something that is enmeshed with the living... We will take that symbol and put it at the center of our kingdom, enclose it with bricks, and pray to it — all together, rather than individually! You may have already guessed that that symbol is a dead body...

But what will we sing? We need to think up a black-vector anthem, something like: "We'll tear *this* world down to its foundation..."

And what will we do? We will probably all work together manufacturing something. Manufacturing what? Weapons, of course, to defend us from our enemies.

So who are our enemies? Those around us, for instance. We will build a huge wall to protect us from all comers.

All of the above is nothing more than the product of a fevered imagination. All coincidences with actual facts, people, and events are purely accidental. To keep you from taking the easiest path, however, I will remind you that the word "mausoleum" comes from the name of the ancient ruler Mausolus (4th century BC), whose tomb in Halicarnassus (today part of Turkey) was considered one of the seven wonders of the ancient world. The first huge wall was built in China, also quite a while ago, so there are more coincidences than it might seem at first glance.

Most important is to remember that there are places on our planet where the black vector in all its destructiveness has long held sway. All of them have seen extensive armed conflict: the Middle East, the Northern Caucasus, Latin America, and the Balkans (the former Yugoslavia). Recent times have seen other areas appear, while the intensity seen in the more long-standing ones is growing. Often you get the feeling we live in a black-vector era.

But there should be some kind of force for good (from the vector point of view) that can stand up to black-vector destructiveness, right? Some claim that power to be people with a combination of the red and blue vectors, which we will soon be discussing. Incidentally, people with that vector pair are sometimes called "indigo children"...

FILMS TO WATCH (WITH BLACK-VECTORED CHARACTERS)

- Forrest Gump, directed by Robert Zemeckis, USA, 1994 (Forrest Gump, played by Tom Hanks)

- Pumping Iron (documentary), directed by George Butler, USA, 1977 (Arnold Schwarzenegger)

- The Terminator, directed by James Cameron, USA, 1984 (Sarah Connor, played by Linda Hamilton)

- Léon: The Professional, directed by Luc Besson, France, 1994 (Léon, played by Jean Reno)

- Million Dollar Baby, directed by Clint Eastwood, USA, 2004 (Maggie Fitzgerald, played by Hilary Swank)

Visit my site www.psy8.net to enjoy the Vector Test, the Vector Gallery (pictures, movies and citations of all eight vectors), the article about the compatibility of vectors, answers to readers' questions, and more.

CHAPTER 5. THE ORANGE VECTOR — SKIN

The time has come to discuss the openings we have scattered all over our bodies. This chapter focuses on the skin and the numerous orifices that make it up: sebaceous and sweat glands, pores, and hair follicles. People who have exceptionally sensitive skin belong to the orange vector, one Viktor Tolkachev referred to as the "dermal" vector.

You can take the Vector Test on my site www.psy8.net

PLEASURES OF THE SKIN

Orange-vectored people loved being gently stroked, especially on their back between their shoulder blades — they could sit for hours enjoying the sensation. Since it can be difficult to find someone willing to keep them happy from morning till night, however, they try to extend the feeling by growing their hair out, tying it back, and letting it gently graze their back. But because our dermal receptors quickly grow accustomed to new sensations, that hair trick only lasts for so long. What else is there to do? Well, some take showers, enjoying the powerful stream of water hitting them. Another option is a steam massage, using gradually stiffer and stronger implements to achieve a strong, head-to-toe dermal orgasm. Once even that becomes old hat, it might be more difficult to think up new tricks. But why make it harder than it has to be? There are still plenty of things to try:

whips, handcuffs, and other sharp objects...

The key is that the body has an "escape" mechanism: it responds to pain by producing a special chemical called endorphins to help deal with that pain. Orange-vectored people produce excess endorphins, not to eliminate the pain entirely, but instead due to a connection between pain and deep psychological pleasure.

Ultimately, when the orange vector is realized and satisfied — it is receiving enough caresses, tenderness, and other dermal pleasures — the person is balanced, gregarious, and well-adapted to life. Sadly, cases with a satisfied orange vector occur only rarely in our time. People most often do not get enough dermal pleasure, something that goes all the way back to their childhood, and instead look for a replacement by subconsciously turning to more painful substitutes.

If this vector is suppressed (not accepted), the person can exhibit a masochistic complex that hunts for both physical and emotional suffering. In the worst case scenario, orange-vectored neurosis, that suffering becomes an entire lifestyle. For example, an orange-vectored girl might purposely marry a man who does not love her, spending her life miserable in that marriage. She might also look for a profession that does not suit her in the least, ending up just as miserable in the workplace. Even worse, people for whom this vector is in neurosis sometimes suffer from skin sores that look awful and itch constantly.

Dissatisfied orange-vectored people simply cannot be happy, as they are the "professionally unfortunate." Just try taking away their unhappiness and watch how they fight to hang onto it!

A girl once asked me, "Why do you think we were born to be happy?" I answered, "I was, at least, but you can think what you want about you…" And off we went down different paths in our lives.

BIORHYTHMS AND TIME

Orange-vectored people have precise biorhythms, with all the biochemical processes in their bodies steady and regular. They are chronometer-esque with their intuitive sense of time even without access to a clock.

How do you find the orange-vectored person in a crowd? Ask a few people to close their eyes and raise their hand when they think a minute has passed. Red-vectored people will be first (at approximately the 30-second mark), as they are always in a hurry to rush on ahead of everyone else. Last will be methodical, slow-paced brown-vectored people (they will raise their hands about 1.5 — 2 minutes later) who are content to watch the world pass them by. However, if you see anyone raise their hand in exactly one minute (give or take), they are orange-vectored. Wondering what happened to your black-vectored friends? They are probably asleep by now…

Thanks to their built-in clock, orange-vectored people are generally on time, though showing up early is not their thing. They simply have everything calculated in advance, even taking unexpected developments into account.

Brown-vectored people are very responsible: they leave home early, though they still manage to get stuck crossing their threshold and therefore are often late. Red-vectored people are generally early or late (they live by the beat of their own drum), and are only on time by pure accident.

If you are even five minutes late to a meeting with an orange-vectored person, do not be surprised if you arrive to find that they did not wait for you. And if they did, expect a lecture on how time is money.

I remember the first time I visited Viktor Tolkachev (his orange vector was fairly strong). Knowing my habit of being late (red and brown vectors), I left home and arrived an hour early. After sitting in the hallway for an hour, I rang his doorbell just as the clock struck six. The happy owner opened the door immediately (he was obviously ready at that exact time as well) and exclaimed, "Well, there's a dermal vector for you!"

Now that you know this orange-vector feature, it is not hard to make orange-vectored people happy. Remember that orange-vectored hosts, having invited their guests to arrive at 6 pm, may very well be washing the floor in some old clothes at 5:55. They will still be ready and dressed at the door at exactly 6 pm, though if you are 5-10 minutes late, they will blame the overcooked meal on you.

NUMBERS AND SAVINGS

Orange-vectored people are not only human clocks; they are also human calculators with a fanatical passion for numbers. Everything gets counted, from stairs to the number of cars in a freight train. They know exactly how much money they have in their wallets down to the last penny.

Red-vectored people are generally clueless: they always have a few wrinkled, differently denominated bills in their wallets they have forgotten about. Then when the season changes and it comes time to pull clothes out of their closets, they often find more money in the pockets. Brown-vectored people, of course, do keep track of their money, though they round off the numbers for simplicity's sake.

Orange-vectored people love doing the counting and measuring themselves, though they also never pass up a chance to double-check those around them — seeing how good their math is and at the same time keeping them honest. That is why orange-vectored people carefully count the change they are given at stores and restaurants, comparing that number to the receipt they were given. This behavior is not neurotic; it is simply a strongly expressed orange vector.

Why do you think a housewife would need a scale in the kitchen? Well, for example, she might use it to weigh ingredients when she is cooking something. Orange-vectored housewives need one for an entirely different reason: when they get home from the store, they pull it out and double-check how much the vegetables they bought weigh. And if they find they were cheated, they are not afraid to march back over and demand the difference. It is thanks to orange-vectored people putting dishonest salesmen in their place that we have as little deception in our lives as we do.

And who needs the scales at stores you can use to check listed weights? Red-vectored people? Of course not! They buy their watermelon, accidentally pay for two, and are none the wiser (they generally leave the receipt at the cash register). Brown-vectored people? No again! They know where the honest salesmen work and only visit them. Black-vectored people? Not at all! It would take too long for them to figure out how the scales work. Instead, they are used by orange-vectored people who even sometimes keep a little weight in their pocket to make sure scales are working correctly. Orange-vectored people from years ago often carried around steelyard balances, a counterweighted scale to counterbalance and measure weight, though they now settle for a calculator and a small tape-measure.

One more thing orange-vectored people enjoy doing regardless of their financial condition is visiting different stores to compare prices.

I know a young woman who goes on an extraordinarily expensive cruise around the world every year, though the rest of the time she scours stores to pay 5% less for her sausage. I once asked her why she needs those savings since she is obviously well off. She answered, "I'm able to take a cruise every year because I don't spend that extra 5% on sausage!"

My own orange vector is strong enough (I always have a calculator with me), and so I decided to figure out how much sausage she would need to eat at that rate to save enough for a cruise. I also tried the same with bread and butter for comparison. It turns out it would take more than a lifetime!

While this behavior is sometimes irrational, it speaks to a lifestyle that is perfect for orange-vectored people of all ages. The most important thing is that they feel good about themselves, and saving a penny here and a penny there is the psychological equivalent of dermal pleasure.

Key words for them are "sale" and "cheap," with many companies running marketing campaigns aimed squarely at orange-vectored people. They also like advertisements built on exact calculations: "Every fourth time you brush your teeth is free!" or "Now wash nine more t-shirts for the same price!"

They love prices that end in a nine, as they like getting both a receipt and at least symbolic change.

Brown-vectored people, on the other hand, hate prices that end in a nine, feeling like someone out there is trying to pull one over on them...

THAT'S MINE!

Orange-vectored people take their property very seriously, subconsciously treating it as an extension of their own bodies. That is why taking something of theirs even temporarily can seriously discomfit them.

An orange-vectored psychologist is running a lesson — he has 18 assignments and 18 paperclips for 18 people. He relaxes, confident in the knowledge that he has enough for everyone, until a red-vectored colleagues without any of his mental baggage rushes in: "Hey, can I grab a paperclip?" Without waiting for an answer, he just picks one up, hurries right back out of the room, and leaves the orange-vectored psychologist hurt and frustrated that he is now missing one paperclip. Of course, he is a regular orange-vectored guy and this is not his first rodeo, so he has some spares. He is still hurt and frustrated though!

As you can probably guess, orange-vectored children dislike sharing their toys. They do often agree to temporary trades, though they are sure to take into account the relative value of the goods at stake: handing over a bike for the chance to play with a shovel will probably not cut it.

Orange-vectored people love keeping track of their finances, writing down all their income and expenses: car, TV, grains, matches, and everything else, all of which goes into a single column. If their budget permits, they pick up some accounting software that does the calculations for them, though some still take the time to double-check everything once a year (usually on April 15). Their preferred tool in that case is the abacus.

FASTING

If the orange vector is not realized or accepted, that passion for savings can take a turn for the worse. One option for orange-vectored masochists is "experimenting" on their own stomachs. Maybe you know the type: "Why are you eating that cheese?! It's still good!" or "Don't eat the fresh bread until we finish the stale loaf. We finish the old one first!" (in the meantime, the fresh bread gets moldy waiting its turn, though it does eventually get eaten).

Ultimately, however, it works even better to simply go hungry. Paul Bragg[8], a well-known orange-vectored American, sometimes went without eating for a day, while other times he fasted for two days or even a week. In that time the orange-vector organism suffers so much that it produces an extraordinary amount of endorphins, enough to last for quite a while. That is why Paul Bragg wrote *The Miracle of Fasting*, in which everything is calculated and scheduled perfectly for the orange vector: when to begin and end, with times and measurements all strictly laid out. It

---

[8] Paul Bragg (1895—1976) is a well-known American figure in alternative medicine, naturopath, healthy-lifestyle propagandist, businessman, and showman. His book *The Miracle of Fasting* enjoyed significant success in the second half of the 20th century.

works something like this: 47 minutes after finishing a fast you eat 94 grams of carrots, moving on to 82 grams of cabbage 23 minutes later. Millions of orange-vectored people the world over have read the book, fasted, and cured dermal and non-dermal diseases alike.

If fasting is too difficult, a strict diet (vegetarian, raw, or one of the myriad other options) is often enough to do the trick.

Some angry people claim that vegetarians could not care less about animals; they simply hate plants...

That is a joke, of course, but I have never once met someone who enjoys fasting or a harsh diet with an only weakly developed orange vector.

Brown-vectored people, by the way, differ from orange-vectored people in that they care about their health but do not resort to diets of that nature: they prefer balanced diets and/or the Hay Diet.

RESERVES

Orange-vectored people serve as the supply agents in the system (family), making sure there is always backup ready. That backup comes in handy during tough times when beggars cannot be choosers and we have to use whatever we have. People with an imbalanced orange vector keep spares that would last through a fifth and sixth life, something that differentiates them from the frugal brown vector.

While brown-vectored people gather mushrooms and berries in the summer, storing them in jars and managing to finish them just as the next summer rolls around, orange-vectored people have a different strategy. They collect as much as they possibly can, storing their harvest on one of the many shelves in their pantry or loft. If you are at a friend's house and are offered five- or even ten-year-old jelly, your friend is definitely orange-vectored (brown-vectored people care too much about their digestive system to eat anything that expired even just last night).

Orange-vectored people are the ones who make pancakes with the cheapest flour they can find, even if they have to go through and pick out the worms first.

While brown-vectored people find a swollen can in their refrigerator and throw it out, orange-vectored people stick it in a pot to boil. The worst thing that could be in that can is the deadly toxin botulism[9]. However, it is killed by long periods at high temperatures, and everything else that survives is not nearly as scary: the worst that could happen is diarrhea. Orange-vectored people, in contrast to their brown-vectored friends, are not afraid of diarrhea, and their motto is, "You can eat anything as long as you heat it up enough first."

For many (and especially red-vectored) people, orange-vector habits like these are incredibly annoying. But just try to remember that some of your ancestors may have survived thanks to such qualities, meaning that you would not exist if it were not for a strong orange vector in your family...

Nearly every orange-vectored person has their "treasure

---

[9] Botulism is a disease caused by eating foods with botulism rods. Preserving foods without access to oxygen leads to the rods multiplying and giving out a toxin that is the strongest bacterial poison on the planet. Interestingly, modern science holds that there *can be no other* more poisonous substance in nature!

box" at home where they keep everything they "need": a piece of razor blade, an empty cartridge from a ballpoint pen, a conveniently long piece of string, a nut of unknown size (maybe one day the bolt will turn up), and much more. New "valuables" are added all the time, though nothing is ever taken out. And when the orange-vectored owner passes on, family members usually leave it out by the curb to be quickly picked through by orange-vectored passers-by.

This vector loves finding and jumping on freebies, though they should not be confused with just anything that is free: orange-vectored people know very well that there is no such thing as a free lunch. Finding an honest-to-goodness freebie takes a *sharp wit*, or being in the right place at the right time.

Orange-vectored people can build their houses using nothing but scraps. They are never prouder than when they can say they did not use a single new nail — what is the point when you can find an old one, straighten it out, and pound it home? Incidentally, they claim that rusty nails hold better. Maybe they are right?

The end of the 20th century featured book after book in countries all over the world following the "thirty useful tips" model, all of which can be found in every orange-vector home. After all, they are founts of information on how to turn trash into treasure. Helpful advice was also featured during TV programs, with millions of orange-vectored people leaning in to find out how to make a backscratcher from an ordinary plastic bottle.

Did you know that you can cut off the end of an empty toothpaste tube and brush your teeth three more times?

The dishes they buy in the current period of their lives usually go unused, saved for the next: when I get married, when I have children, or when I have grandchildren. For now, orange-vectored people eat from a chipped plate and drink from a carefully glued cup.

"Who cares that the teapot spout leaks? Don't fill it all the way and it'll work just fine."

LITTLE GATHERERS

These same orange-vector abilities appear at a very young age. Orange-vectored children are always on the prowl for things they can find a use for at home, and they are always more than happy to pocket things that are poorly hidden: someone else's toy, for example. At home a brown-vectored mother who is honest to a fault might shout at one of them, "You thief! They used to cut hands off for that!" On the one hand, that mom is completely right: it is wrong to take things that do not belong to you. On the other, that overly emotional response can instill a "penniless complex" in the child. The ability to take what life offers, after all, is crucial for the orange vector's financial happiness.

What could that mother have done differently? Every "no" needs to be accompanied by a "yes," teaching children not to take things that do not belong to them while also showing them how to honestly reach their potential. For example, they can go pick mushrooms and berries or bring something else home without stealing from anyone.

Once when I was in second grade our natural sciences teacher showed us a piece of granite. She talked about how the beautiful stone was used to build monuments, subway stations, and many other fascinating things, and we really were entranced by the way it glistened in the sun. A week later my buddy and I were walking after school when we saw a huge pile next to the road. What do you think it was? Granite! And there was nobody nearby.

I ran over to it, picked up one rock, and said to my friend, "Look, it's granite!" "Granite?" he answered, unfazed. "We need to take it!" I said shouted. And so we started packing it into our backpacks. However, there was not much space thanks to the books and notepads we had absolutely no use for at the moment, and so I started shoveling granite into my pack with the extra pair of shoes I had with me. Once there was no more room, we started hauling our treasure to my house for some reason. The pack with its new load was very heavy, forcing me to drag it along the last three hundred feet of asphalt. Ultimately, however, all that was nothing compared to how excited I was about my "treasure."

I burst into the apartment shouting, "Mom, dad, look what I brought!" and dumping it all on the floor. And that all hell broke loose: my parents were horrified, screeching, "Are you an idiot?! Your grandmother made you that bag! And now look how you dragged it through the dirt and tore it! Get all this out of the house and into the trash immediately." There was nothing to do but toss all my granite into the trash and ask my grandmother's forgiveness for the torn bag. It has been 35 years since then, but I still remember it like it was yesterday. I even had to work through the experience during a psychology seminar to keep that traumatic childhood event from ruining how I felt about money.

In short, be careful how you deal with children who take what does not belong to them without thinking. If the child is handed down an unreasonably harsh punishment, she may develop a habit of lying that will only complicate things.

If orange-vectored people do not get through their "collector" stage in childhood with balance and acceptance, they can turn to kleptomania (a habit of minor theft) as adults. Some of them are convinced that stolen flowers grow better, and so they tear branches off plants that catch their eye whenever possible. Others think books that do not belong to them are more interesting to read, which is why you need to keep an eye on them when they stop by for a visit or head over to the library. Some people cannot leave a restaurant without taking a spoon or wine glass as a souvenir, to say nothing of hotel rooms: shampoo, soap, and shower caps are only for beginners. Amateurs walk out with bed linens, towels, and robes, and they themselves do not even compare to the "professionals."

Remember the "rule of S" to avoid accusations of theft at hotels. Most hotels do not care if you take anything that begins with the letter S:

This way of life is so natural for many orange-vectored people that they cannot imagine how other people could live differently. That is why the people around them think of them as thieves: "If my things aren't where they belong, they were stolen!" The washbasin with a hole in it was stolen, the torn galoshes were stolen, and the garden shed is a prime target, so it is important to check every week to make sure everything is there.

PRESENTS

Orange-vectored people generally do not give flowers — why spend so much money on something that will be dead tomorrow? If they absolutely have to buy flowers for someone, they prefer to give a potted plant that will last longer. And they certainly do not get green-vectored people and their fleeting enthusiasm that is stronger for a beautiful bouquet of flowers than even the most valuable gift. Orange-vectored people think the best present is an envelope full of cash.

Incidentally, some orange-vectored people do not like getting presents, as it makes them feel like they are indebted to the giver. They start wondering why they have to give something in return.

When I was young I had a friend who came to my birthday parties every year. One time he gave me a great book I enjoyed reading immensely: Robert Louis Stevenson's Treasure Island. I do not remember what he gave me the next year, but the one after that he gave me another book. And guess what? It was the same Treasure Island! I put them together on the shelf and he walked by multiple times that evening without noticing a thing. No matter, it would be pretty easy to forget something after a couple years — but a year later he gave me a third copy! I had to tell him: "You know, I already have two of these..." My friend was not embarrassed in the least, and answered, "Well, now you have three." His parents probably picked up an entire box of the lovely books and were giving them to everyone, though their lack of a brown vector meant they were not keeping track of who had already received a copy.

Orange-vectored people do not have to rush around on Christmas Eve because everything has long since been bought. They spend the entire year looking for sales, buying in bulk to make sure they have enough for everyone. While they are usually careful to remove the price tag so as to make sure nobody knows their present was bought on sale, they do sometimes buy more expensive gifts to demonstrate their status or show the strong relationship they have with the recipient. In that case they may even stick the price tag onto the top of the box or highlight it with a marker.

The other side of the coin is that giving orange-vectored people gifts without price tags means putting them through the ringer. Now they have to go shopping to figure out how much your present cost so they know how much they owe you. For the same reason, avoid giving people like this gifts that are too expensive — they will worry about not being able to "repay" you.

Orange-vectored people can be completely serious when they give their children a nickel and tell them to go buy whatever they want.

PACKRATS

Orange-vectored people stuff themselves when visiting friends, even if they are on a diet at home. They sometimes even bring a bag or container with them to take home what they cannot eat there.

On the other hand, they prefer not to entertain, especially staying away from yellow-vectored gluttons and their terrible table manners. You will never see a salad bowl or meat dish on the table in an orange-vector home; everything is evenly portioned out in the kitchen. And if you forget yourself and ask for seconds, get ready for a gentle reminder that there is a McDonalds around the corner.

Orange-vectored hosts sometimes let slip how much dinner cost or say something like, "Go ahead, dig in — this is all we have left." They buy two packs of ten sausages when they are expecting ten people (exactly two per person), and worry about an eleventh person coming — buying a third pack for just one more person makes no sense whatsoever.

Think back to the last time you read Sleeping Beauty — what happened? There was no set of utensils for the eighth fairy! The problem was that the orange-vectored host had no desire to get another set from the pantry, at which point the fairy, who happened to be violet-vectored, took full revenge on the hapless host!

In some orange-vectored families with birthdays just a week or two away from Christmas, they just reuse the leftovers from the first celebration.

Orange-vectored people hang onto old instructions for

years, even after the appliances they belong to have long since been thrown out or picked apart. This vector rejects the use of the phrase "to throw out" (negatively significant).

"This pot has gone through three moves with me, and you're saying I should throw it out??"

If orange-vectored people do not get enough of the pleasure their skin craves, their passion for collecting gets even worse. Spacious homes and apartments sprout cabinets and shelves from every which way to store things "just in case." In the end, you can only walk through them sideways.

Brown-vectored people are also notable for their frugality, though they do not hold onto things they do not need and throw out instructions along with their appliances.

Orange-vectored people love computers and especially the Recycle Bin, which is a place to send "deleted" things that are never really deleted. Accidentally clicking "Empty Recycle Bin" is the same for them as accidentally reformatting their hard drive. Their computers lack a set structure; instead, several folders with moderately important documents share space with highly sensitive folders in the Archive. Everything is saved from the moment the first computer is bought, including, if you dig deep enough, quite a few sets of instructions on what to do about Y2K[10].

---

[10] Y2K, or the Year 2000 problem, occurred because software developed in the 19th century used digit pairs to indicate dates: January 1, 1961, became 01.01.61. Once January 1, 2000 (01.01.00), rolled around, quite a few old programs interpreted it as January 1, 1900, something that many worried would lead to major breakdowns.

APPEARANCE AND HABITS

Long hair tied back into a ponytail is typical for the orange vector, and even for orange-vectored men. Other hairstyles are chosen for the savings they create by needing a haircut only twice a year. Incidentally, redheads often have a strong orange vector.

Balanced orange-vectored people have very sensitive, velvety skin, and they love stroking it and their hair. In stressful situations they often scratch themselves.

People like this often have thin, sometimes pinched lips. They speak with an instructive tone, matching it with the way they wave their finger around: "I'll show you" (as they point into the air or tap on the table).

Orange-vectored people dress practically and economically, loving thrift stores and not being afraid to patch up old clothes. In families with several children, the youngest rarely gets any new clothes. In spite of their economy, however, they particularly enjoy leather and fur (fluffy) things.

Their favorite color is orange, and their symbol is the cross or plus sign.

Orange-vectored people enjoy contrast showers, swimming in icy water, acupuncture, and acupressure mats. They are also big fans of crossword puzzles, all kinds of logic games, and training people (their own family, their own children, or other people's children).

Their handwriting is small and scrunched, with sharp characters. When writing letters they try to fill up the entire page without leaving any open areas ("luxuries" like paragraph breaks and indentations are out the window). For unimportant documents like those same letters they choose the cheapest paper they can find.

Quite a few years back a seminar participant brought a note written by his father-in-law that became a fixture of lessons on the orange vector:

"Thanks a ton for partially washing the dishes. It would be nice if you could finish the job — I like using the pot and pan that are out on the balcony. I'm also hoping you'll take out the trash. Although you put the iron away (progress!), you should have done the same with the blanket and plug from the lamp after you used the hairdryer.

That's all for now. I imagine you'll spend more time reading this letter than you spent on all the colossal work you did. Let's not make a mountain out of a molehill, okay?

P.S. Don't eat the sour cream, etc. I'm on a diet and have neither the means nor the desire at the moment to feed you."

While black-vectored people live in constant contact with their bodies, orange-vectored people feel the same about the world around them (they sense it through their skin). Balanced orange-vectored people live healthy lives and love all different types of exercise, from jogging to rhythmic gymnastics to even yoga. With that said, saunas occupy a special place in their hearts. For them they are less a hygienic exercise and more a separate world with its own culture, unusual sensations, and completely different way of talking. Telling an orange-vectored person you do not enjoy saunas has the same effect as talking to red-vectored people about the past or brown-vectored people about the future: you will end up with one less friend. Incidentally, a dislike for saunas can be a sign of an unaccepted orange vector.

Orange-vectored people and their highly sensitive skin cannot stand creased sheets or crumbs in the bed. Believe it or not, a friend of mine could not go to sleep until he got the tennis ball out from under his bed — and it was not even touching the mattress! Their sensitivity obviously extends far beyond bodily contact.

Some orange-vectored men prefer to shave frequently, even twice a day, as they find it to be great for their skin. Others, on the other hand, prefer not to, as their skin is easily irritated. Those in the latter camp only shave once every week (or two), though always on the same day — orange-vectored people are creatures of habit. So if your colleague is only clean-shaven on Mondays (or on Mondays and Thursdays), you can be sure he has a strong orange vector.

They love taking showers, and especially contrast showers (note that red-vectored people prefer baths or pools, where there is much more water).

Orange-vectored people adore massages, though instead of deep tissue massages they like superficial ones that are only skin-deep (black-vectored people are the ones who prefer strong, deep massages where the masseuse "adjusts your spine via your stomach").

Many orange-vectored people love cats, which are pleasant to the touch even when short-haired. The most important ditch to avoid, however, is "old cat lady" syndrome: they lived long and happy lives, dying on the same day.

While brown-vectored people tidy up to make sure their

houses are clean (getting to the dirt in all the nooks and crannies), orange-vectored people only do so for discipline's sake (if you cannot see it, it is not there).

Orange-vectored people are generally not charitable, convinced as they are that free hand-outs are evil. They also find it very difficult to give bribes, though they have fewer qualms accepting them.

A son walks up to his father and says, "Dad, today I dreamed you gave me a little chocolate bar!" The father calmly replies, "If you behave, you'll be dreaming about how I gave you a big chocolate bar next."

A peculiarity native to the orange vector is a practicality that insists on everything having its own meaning, use, or benefit. Existential crises occur only rarely, as orange-vectored people do not think too deeply about the meaning of life or the philosophy of being. On the other hand, they are unparalleled (even among black-vectored people) in their endurance: they would last the longest on a deserted island in the cold, without food, and almost without water. Their motto is: "Suffer everything, make it through all trials, and survive." That survival instinct may be what kept many alive along the long Oregon Trail or in the German concentration camps.

DISCIPLINE

Orange-vectored people are human clocks, so discipline for them is a joy. The organization they instill in all areas of their lives is the envy of the other vectors, and especially the red vector.

Orange-vectored children display these qualities from the day they are born, easily fitting into required schedules: they sleep the given number of hours, eat exactly as much as they are supposed to, and do everything by the book. Being a parent to one of them is generally a walk in the park, as they behave exactly how parenting guides say they will. In contrast to red-vectored children, orange-vectored ones feel uncomfortable when they have too much freedom in their lives and need structure. Without it they feel uneasy and sometimes begin to manifest skin disorders.

At school orange-vectored children make great students, earning top grades with their trademark discipline (incidentally, orange-vectored children are the only ones who can be incentivized to study using money).

Their love of discipline only grows stronger with age — a daily regime is set and followed strictly for years. Every day they wake up at the same time without an alarm clock (remember, they have an internal clock), eat the same breakfast (nutritious and economic), take the same road to work, and do the same job. They also have a daily workout routine and/or take a cold shower daily. Their lives move along a predetermined plan: this year they are buying a TV, next year a car, and in three years a house. And that is how it happens.

Orange-vector qualities make these people irreplaceable in the workplace during times when the red-vectored leader has to be away. The orange-vectored replacement, of course, is not capable of carrying the team on her shoulders, though she is more than able to organize everyone according to a plan already in place and instill strict discipline. That is often enough to keep the team moving forward and together until the red-vectored leader gets back.

Their love of discipline pushes orange-vectored people into careers as teachers, where they make sure rule-keeping and other standards are highly prioritized. A clear hierarchy of teachers and students is also important for them.

How do orange-vectored teachers generally do their job? "Okay, you little mongrels, today you learn how to raise your hands: get 'em up exactly to the tip of your ear. Got it? Let's see what you can do." In the back row, of course, a red-vectored student has no tolerance for rules in his life. "You bring your parents to school tomorrow so I can tell them how to raise an obedient child."

Orange-vectored people do their best to make sure everyone on earth knows how to behave. Their favorite words and phrases are "have to," "required," and "rules." People like that are fanatically committed to the idea of duty: "duty above all." But what is more important than duty? Money, of course. The most duty-bound orange-vectored person still has a number they cannot resist. It may be quite high, but there definitely is one — and the person mostly likely knows (or guesses) what it is. Never think of orange-vectored people as 100% principled, as the right sum may simply not yet have been offered.

PROFESSIONS AND THE WORKPLACE

The main advantage orange-vectored people enjoy is a stunning sense of logic they can apply to widely varying areas of their lives. They are drawn to all professions related to numbers and money: mathematician, cashier, accountant, economist, financier, and so on. Remember that the best accountant is a mix of the orange and brown vectors (if the latter is missing, the firm may occasionally find itself missing significant sums).

Among other professions and hobbies they prefer sports that focus on endurance and accuracy: marathons, fencing, biathlon, rhythmic gymnastics, figure skating, ballet, and ballroom dancing. They are also often found at supervisory and inspection agencies working as controllers, auditors, epidemiologists, epidemic response station workers, fire prevention specialists, and tax specialists.

In the workplace orange-vectored people follow instructions exactly and do not show any particular enthusiasm for their job. They finish work precisely on time — "no one's paying me to stay later" — and love hourly pay or even being paid by the minute, which makes calculations easier.

I remember once how we hired an orange-vectored babysitter for our child. At the end of the day she calculated what we owed her and said, "I worked five hours and seven minutes, so you owe me $51.17." Smiling, she went on, "But don't worry about the 17 cents." And finally, without any embarrassment whatsoever, "I'll add them in next time."

While red-vectored people are inventors who design complete novelties, orange-vectored people are able to think up ways to use old things more profitably.

People with a weak red vector and strong orange vector are not big earners. Red-vectored people are the ones who take risks, investing all their money, losing it, earning some more, investing their new savings, and finally raking in a fortune. Orange-vectored people never risk everything; they spread their money across different accounts in different banks, losing a little here, gaining a little there, and in the end coming out with modest, if guaranteed growth.

Be sure to lay out all the terms and conditions ahead of time down to the last penny before starting to work with a person like this. Remember: orange-vectored people are not volunteers — you have to pay them.

LOVE AND SEX

Orange-vectored people have middling sexual potential. If their vector is not satisfied, they may fall hopelessly in love, perhaps with someone from a book or one of their friends' partners. Here the subconscious goal is to suffer, seeing as how imbalanced orange-vector love often appears as deep suffering (think here of Dostoevsky's characters).

Marriage to a person like this, of course, is built on calculations: orange-vectored people may hold off on a marriage for a week to see if anything better turns up. Prenuptial agreements are obviously the great masterpiece of the orange vector.

Sex in such a marriage happens strictly on schedule: for example, on Tuesdays and Fridays at 10 pm.

An orange-vectored man comes home and tells his wife: "Mary, get ready!" She thinks to herself, "What happened?! Today is Wednesday!" Happily, she grabs a quick shower and jumps excitedly into bed, which is when he enters, fully dressed, and says, "April fool's! Ha-ha-ha…"

That is the kind of humor orange-vectored people enjoy: nothing terribly funny, and more like a chill running across your skin. They say traditional English humor elicits a similar reaction.

Orange-vectored men have long since calculated that the average man is capable of achieving 56,742 orgasms over the course of his life. And given that his ejaculate is important to the female organism, he prefers not to waste it, which is why you need to encourage orange-vectored men in the bedroom. That encouragement does not need to be monetary; it can be little gifts (pens or paperclips) or making a little treat. Regardless, it is also important to say something like, "This is just a little thank you for the wonderful night." Orange-vectored women are the same way: they sometimes are even more turned on when paid for sex, even by their own husband.

Two orange-vectored people married to each other live happy lives: they have separate budgets, separate shelves in the refrigerator (or separate refrigerators), and they go to the sauna, go swimming in icy water, go running, and fast together. Life is also a competition to see who can get better deals — the one who wins is usually the one who happens across the freebie.

RELATING TO PEOPLE

Orange-vectored people care deeply about what the people around them think, and they spend inordinate amounts of time and energy making sure their families meet social standards and fit within social frameworks. "What will the neighbors think?!" is something an orange-vectored mother or grandmother might say.

Friendships with orange-vectored people are built on usefulness, and they end once that usefulness is exhausted. On the other hand, their friends are generally not aware that they are being used, as orange-vectored people are able to act in their own interests without anyone noticing.

They love offering advice, try to teach people how to live their lives, and sometimes guilt trip the people around them (especially their children): "I raised you, went days without sleeping for you, and this is how you repay me..."

Another way orange-vectored people manipulate others is by insisting on helping, only to later call in that favor: "Here, let me help you. I don't mind, and you look like you could really use it." You feel pressured to accept, but a couple weeks later your orange-vectored friend comes over and says, "You remember what I did for you?! Do you have any idea what it cost me?!"

The orange vector has one more interesting quality: orange-vectored people adore speaking plainly. However, that has nothing to do with, for instance, the brown vector's honesty and fairness. "Sweetie, I have no idea who you got that mug of yours from! Hey, what's the matter? If your mother doesn't tell you the truth, who will?"

Be sure to uphold all the monetary and time commitments you make to orange-vectored people when dealing with them, remembering that they are always aware of the exact balance owed in each individual relationship. If you think there may be an issue with the accounting, do your best to get it fixed immediately. Ultimately, try not to accept money or things from orange-vectored people — after all, "if you want to lose a friend, lend him money (or borrow money from him)."

Dissatisfied orange-vectored people love complaining about their lives: "all the other lines are moving faster" or "all the good produce always runs out right when I get there."

HEALTH

Realized and satisfied orange vectors generally do not create any health problems. On the other end, orange-vectored people with suppressed vectors or vectors in neurosis may suffer from skin diseases. Generally speaking, all skin diseases can be traced back to an imbalanced orange vector: even newborns can have theirs suppressed and develop skin diseases while they are still nursing.

Orange-vectored people in neurosis scratch themselves a lot and refuse to be caressed. If your friend warns you not to touch him, you can be absolutely sure he is in orange-vector neurosis.

Dissatisfied orange-vectored people also love complaining about their health, sometimes spending months visiting doctors in search of reasons for their poor condition. Their doctors, however, can never find anything seriously wrong with them.

Orange-vectored people are self-fulfilling prophesies on two legs: if they read in the newspaper that tomorrow will be an unsuccessful day, you can be sure they will have a bad day tomorrow. Even if that newspaper turns out to be from last year, they will have a bad day on the date they saw in it. This makes them different from blue-vectored people, who are not impressionable and instead are weather-sensitive — they have bad days when bad days are fated to happen, regardless of what the newspaper says.

Orange-vectored people love treatments like acupuncture, leeches, ants, cold or hot water, and, of course, fasting. They need to be careful when tanning, as their sensitive skin burns quickly.

PATHWAY TO LOVE

Many people start to look down on orange-vectored people after learning about this vector. To be honest, after Viktor Tolkachev's "dermal" lesson I had a similar feeling. As I was still prone to sharp judgements, I decided that orange-vectored people are the unpleasant ones I saw around me and that I was nothing like them. It was no coincidence that my orange vector at the time was only 13% (thirteen percent!) accepted.

However, a few weeks or months later the scales fell from my eyes, I examined my life, and I found something that surprised me. It turned out that the number of orange-vector qualities I displayed was almost as many as the ones Tolkachev talked about at that lesson, while it was only that initial negativity that kept me from seeing that the orange vector is my strongest.

Here are just a few examples of what I saw. When I was 16 I tried fasting for 2-3 days (I do not know why — perhaps just to see what I was made of). At the same time I made a habit of dousing myself in cold water (something I have hated ever since I was a child) and running in the morning (I hate running even more). I had my old black and white TVs sitting around my house for years, even after they had all been replaced by color models. I wore the same coat for 14 years, loved money, and thought the best gift was the kind you get in an envelope. While I did not cut the end of toothpaste tubes off, that was only because I had little clamps that served that same purpose even better. My heart would jump into my throat whenever I had to throw something old or spoiled away. And you already know the story about the granite...

Even with all that I would have fought anyone who "accused" me of being orange-vectored. I have no idea how I got through that neurosis without developing any skin diseases! Now, of course, I have been able to accept all of my qualities, making them much more balanced. This vector is one of my strongest, and it was the one I used in my own life to learn how to accept vectors in general. I can now say that I am orange-vectored, and, perhaps more strongly, that orange-vectored is who I am.

FILMS TO WATCH (WITH ORANGE-VECTORED CHARACTERS)

- The Piano Teacher, directed by Michael Haneke; Austria, France, and Germany; 2001 (Erika Kohut, played by Isabelle Huppert)

- A Christmas Carol, directed by Robert Zemeckis; USA; 2009 (Ebenezer Scrooge, played by Jim Carrey)

Visit my site www.psy8.net to enjoy the Vector Test, the Vector Gallery (pictures, movies and citations of all eight vectors), the article about the compatibility of vectors, answers to readers' questions, and more.

CHAPTER 6. THE YELLOW VECTOR — MOUTH

ALL ABOUT THAT FOOD

Ever since some of us were born, all the immense number of receptors in our mouth that measure taste as well as temperature, pain, and touch have been particularly sensitive. Our system assigns this kind of person to the yellow vector, one Viktor Tolkachev referred to as the "oral" vector.

You can take the Vector Test on my site www.psy8.net

How do yellow-vectored people get satisfaction from their significant zone? First and foremost by eating delicious and varying foods. That second adjective is italicized for a reason: everyone remembers how yellow-vectored people like eating food that tastes good, though they sometimes forget how important variety is to them.

People like this are artists with their tongues, able to differentiate between the slightest hints of flavor. Tolkachev used to say that if you put ten unmarked bottles of beer on the table in front of him, he could try them all and tell you exactly which kind was which. He would even be able to tell you when each bottle had been brewed. And that is no exaggeration: yellow-vectored people can lean on their exquisite taste memory to remember practically everything they have ever eaten or drunk, sometimes going back to early childhood. For example, I can remember the taste of the potatoes my grandfather used to fry 30 years ago as if it were yesterday. I think many of you can think of similar instances.

Yellow-vectored people also have good *taste perception*, meaning that they can select a cut of meat at the store and already know how it will taste once cooked.

Given their skill in the kitchen, however, everything non-yellow-vectored people try to concoct in their territory is comparative slop. That is why yellow-vectored people head in that direction to whip something up for themselves whenever they have a spare minute. They have their special salt and other spices, and every new culinary experience is delicious and novel. And, of course, cookbooks are useless when you can just follow your tongue — better save them for light reading on the couch after a good meal.

Cooking for yellow-vectored people is an intimate act (even more so than sex) they only share with those whom they absolutely trust. If one tells you to go watch TV while he cooks something, there is still a barrier of some sort between the two of you...

While black-vectored people eat a ton of the same thing, yellow-vectored people chow down on a smorgasbord of different foods in a specific order. Like notes strung together to form a composition, they look at ingredients as things to be mixed and matched to make an "oral symphony." People with a strong yellow vector know exactly what order to follow when eating — a yellow-vectored husband might divorce a wife who serves fish after meat once the spasms in his tongue go away.

By the same token, yellow-vectored people may not like

salads made by other people, as real salads are works of art made up of a precise fusion of tastes. The perfect potato salad (just like any other dish) cannot be made from a recipe, since so much depends on the flavor offered by each individual ingredient: 400 grams of one kind of potato is perfect, while yellow-vectored chefs recognize instantly that more than 350 grams of another kind would spoil the overall effect. As a result, they prefer eating salads made by other people piece by piece: first the tomatoes, then the cucumbers, and finally the lettuce straight from the head.

The way they act around food can sometimes seem strange: for instance, they love eating with their fingers, almost as if they have taste buds there too. Licking their plate after a meal (when no one is watching) is also a favorite activity, and they like drinking beer and lemonade straight from the bottle — "You lose half the taste when you pour it out."

RARE MEAT

Many yellow-vectored people love sweets, some prefer spicy foods, and others go for more exotic dishes. More than anything, however, yellow-vectored people love meat! Their favorite is meat roasted to rare perfection.

Their nearly animal passion for meat occasionally leads to a subconscious "cannibalism," such as when the aunt comes to visit her nephew and chatters excitedly at him, "Oh, you're so adorable! I could eat you up!" At times like those you can be sure she has a hungry yellow vector. I had an aunt like that who would even bite me lightly — I was terrified of her, running and hiding under the couch whenever she came to visit.

Of course, yellow-vectored people, from children to adults, love biting. However, if you let children like that bite as much as they want, the phase will eventually pass (or at least become much less pronounced). Adults bite the object of their passion to demonstrate love and affection, though they sometimes have even scarier ways of showing their feelings…

Once upon a time a colleague told me about a patient he had. She came and complained about her husband: "My husband' such a thorough blood-sucker I feel exhausted all the time." She came back a week later and repeated her story: "He's all over me, the blood-sucker…" Another week went by and she had the same thing to say, only the doctor, tired of hearing it, asked, "So does he drink a lot of your blood?" "A glassful every time!" It turns out the husband made a habit of biting open her veins and drinking her blood…

In medicine this phenomenon is referred to as clinical vampirism — in this case, of course, a serious psychological disorder. In regular yellow-vector life, however, this love of blood takes a less menacing form: perhaps simply licking up the blood that appears when someone cuts themselves.

There is also a widespread Hollywood cliché where a man is using an open razor to shave with his woman around. She begs him to let her try shaving him, though her inexperience leads to a small cut and a drop of blood that she then licks off. They usually rush to the bedroom soon afterwards.

Try imagining what a mix of strong black and yellow vectors would look like, especially if they were both in neurosis. Pretty complicated…

Incidentally, the first oral pleasure yellow-vectored babies enjoy is sucking on their mother's breast. Regardless of how large it actually is, to the baby that breast looks enormous, leading to a strong mental link between large breasts and pleasure. Men generally fixate on women with that silhouette, and even women prefer thicker men who have something to bite on. Yellow-vectored people (both men and women), as it turns out, almost always prefer fuller figures in the opposite gender.

WAGGING TONGUES

Yellow-vectored people enjoy satisfying their taste buds with a variety of delicious foods. However, that still leaves their tactile receptors needing pleasure. Would you say people giving beautiful speeches in public are actually working? Of course not — they are first and foremost savoring an almost sexual pleasure, as speaking for yellow-vectored people is a form of oral masturbation. They do their best to maximize that pleasure by talking often and at length.

All major companies have that one employee who is always wandering around looking for someone to talk to. Once they find someone, they grab them by a button, pull them off to the side, and tell them two set phrases. The first is, "this'll just take a minute." The second is, "maybe you don't care, but I'll tell you anyway." When that happens, get ready, because the next half hour on your calendar is now full. Of course, people only care to listen to what they find interesting, and so yellow-vectored people have hundreds of stories, the most important of which are the latest gossip. Yellow-vectored people are hysterically funny and the heart of every party. They speak emotionally, with well-formed and rich language that includes a multitude of sayings and tropes.

Two friends meet. The first says to the other, "You know, my wife is quite the orator! She can talk for hours about anything." The other answers, "Lucky you. My wife can talk for hours about absolutely nothing."

Because yellow-vectored people are so passionate about talking, it is nearly impossible for them to keep government, corporate, or personal secrets. Some important organizations are well aware of that fact, and so they pull people like this into a dark room and whisper, "I have a secret for you: there's going to be a bank crisis soon. Just don't tell anyone!" What do they hear in response? "Of course, not a word! Loose lips!", though three days later the entire country is abuzz with the news. Creating rumors and gossip is a powerful tool thought up by federal services to exploit people with strong yellow vectors.

Yellow-vector talkativeness has nothing to do with how loyal yellow-vectored people are or are not to those around them; they might very well want to keep a corporate secret for their favorite company. The problem is that their tongue works faster than their brain, making it just too easy to spill the beans to a "random" acquaintance over a meal.

You may have noticed that yellow-vectored people have a lot in common with their red-vectored friends (vivacity, energy, and sociability). Being red-vectored has its advantages, too: charisma, strong sexual potential, and high social status. That is why yellow-vectored people often "simulate" the red vector in an attempt to be like them: "I'll lead you into the future! We'll move mountains together!" Many people believe them too, and even get on board with their grandiose plans: "We're ready — lead us!" But how does the yellow-vectored person respond? "Okay, you go on ahead for now while I have lunch."

How can you tell the difference between yellow-vectored and red-vectored people? When speaking, they are identical, both energetic and inspirational like true leaders. But! Red-vectored people follow speech with action (they may not complete that action, but that is a separate issue), while yellow-vectored people head straight to a meal. Also remember that people can have both vectors: Fidel Castro[11] is a great example.

PROFESSIONS AND THE WORKPLACE

Nature itself made the yellow vector perfect for working with food, and so yellow-vectored people are excellent chefs, tasters, and sommeliers[12] (the violet vector's sense of smell is important for that last one).

There is also no one better suited for professions heavy on speaking: lecturers, dictators, variety actors, interpreters, and tour guides.

---

[11] Fidel Castro is a Cuban leader who holds the Guinness Book of Records title for the longest speech ever delivered at the United Nations: on September 29, 1960, he spoke for all of 4.5 hours. According to Reuters, Castro's longest speech was given at the III Communist Party Congress in 1986 and lasted more than seven hours.

[12] A sommelier is the person at a restaurant responsible for purchasing, storing, and serving wine to the patrons. We will talk more about them in the chapter dealing with the violet vector.

Yellow-vectored people also make fantastic facilitators[13], as they are capable of motivating many people to do a variety of things — including getting them to make purchases. However, regardless of their persuasive abilities, strongly yellow-vectored people are rarely good salesmen, as all their oratorical talents cannot compensate for their inability to listen. There is simply too much of them in the conversation: they become the center of attention and sometimes forget that other people would also like to chime in. Clients, after all, like it when salesmen ask them questions and listen attentively to the answers...

The ideal time for yellow-vector potential to flourish in any company is during brainstorming sessions. Here the pure quantity of ideas they contribute, do not forget, and are able to reason through has no equal. Of course, yellow-vectored people think their job is done once the meeting is over and it is time to get down to work.

People like this are most productive when doing something related to talking, generating ideas, or preparing food; they tend to be lazy when it comes to anything else. If their potential is not needed and they have no outlet for what they love, they risk becoming just another gofer. In that case they spend all their time drinking tea or coffee (and distracting their coworkers) before heading off for a quick smoke, after which they start all over again.

Yellow-vectored people do their best to find the path of least resistance, risking as little as possible and striving for a carefree,

---

[13] A facilitator is a person who makes sure everyone in a given group is communicating well by setting up a relaxed atmosphere and profitable discussion, making the entire process a pleasure for everyone involved.

comfortable existence. They freely and easily drift through life, finding happiness for themselves and those around them. When they happen into a position of power (in a country or organization), they feel like they made an unforgivable error by forgetting the main meaning in their life: enjoyment.

APPEARANCE AND OTHER FEATURES

Yellow-vectored people are rarely slender, more often finding themselves with an average or somewhat heavier build (being significantly overweight, incidentally, can be a sign of yellow-vector neurosis). They have large, nimble mouths, while their puffy, sensitive lips sometimes hide the most distinctive yellow-vector trait there is: protruding canines.

They are also not very tidy, meaning that traces of the food and drink they are constantly consuming while simultaneously having lively conversations can often be found later on their clothes.

The bright colors they wear highlight their cheerfulness, though they are not particularly fashion-conscious. There is no typical hairstyle for this vector.

Yellow-vectored people are very animated and love exaggerated gestures, including stroking their own stomach (after a filling meal), biting and licking their lips, and sticking out their tongue.

They love shouting loudly, be that "DE-FENSE, DE-FENSE" or "hooray!" at a sports game, or at home in the kitchen.

When people like this yell, it does not necessarily mean that they are very angry; it is just how they express emotion. They even tend to generate a shockwave that quite literally throws the person they are talking to against the nearest wall. Yellow-vectored people shout, let off steam, and calm down immediately. "Wow, that's yelling for you..." "I wasn't yelling; I was speaking loudly. You'll know when I start yelling!"

If they cannot yell, they can at least whistle; and if they cannot whistle, they can cluck their tongues — another form of oral masturbation.

YELLOW-VECTORED CHILDREN

Yellow-vectored children are always trying to express themselves. Their verbal intellect[14] is their superpower, and they even think better while talking. A little boy might come home from kindergarten: "Mommy, mommy!" "Go talk to your father." "Daddy, daddy!" "Go talk to your mother"... And just imagine blue-vectored parents (their ears are their sensitive orifices), for whom nothing beats the soothing sound of silence. Their yellow-vectored child runs back and forth between them with no one willing to listen, choking on the words as it were. Children in that situation often end up with a stutter.

Of course, heading out into the neighborhood is a recourse when no one is listening at home, though people there only listen to what they find interesting. "At kindergarten they don't give us anything to eat ever!" The orange- or brown-vectored mother

---

[14] Verbal intellect is the ability to speak artfully, interact with other people, and handle communication issues, in addition to a predilection for the humanities and languages.

happens to hear and responds, "Oh, really? Why don't we go talk to your teacher and you can tell her what you just said. No? So you were lying? Here, this will make you remember not to lie!" And with that she smacks him on the lips. Sure, he will not lie again, but he will also spend his entire life stuttering.

It is important to remember that yellow-vectored children do not really lie; they just make things up. There is nothing for them to gain personally from their fibs, which are spoken with the sole intent of getting people to listen. If real life is not interesting enough, they resort to their imagination.

Yellow-vectored adults behave the same way: when they do not have enough actual details for a good story, they embellish it in a way that has no ulterior motive (the same cannot be said of the elaborate lies weaved by the violet vector).

Of course, speaking is not the only way to get the oral zone going. If your child spends a lot of time with his pacifier, bites his nails, or sleeps with a bit of food in his cheek, it does not mean that he has bad manners. He is just looking for ways to get enjoyment from his significant zone. Keeping him from them when he is young means that when he gets older he will smoke cigarettes or a pipe, stick matches or grass in his mouth, or something else. Incidentally, children who have a hard time giving up their pacifiers are not getting enough oral enjoyment.

I remember one instructive story a mother once told me about her son. He was still sucking on a pacifier at three years of age, while her strong brown vector was very afraid he would drop it on the floor and get an infection. Without the ability to handle the problem head-on, she kept up a running skirmish with her son: every day she would take away the pacifier one minute sooner (today he would have it for 20 minutes, tomorrow for 19, the next day for 18, and so on). Ultimately, nothing worked, as her clever son was always able to win back the minutes he lost.

The mother figured out a creative approach during a vector training seminar. She fastened the pacifier to a wall in the hallway right at the level of the boy's mouth and told him he could suck on it as much as he wanted. Her son was so happy he stood there sucking away for a whole hour while the mother waited with bated breath to see what would happen next...

Afterwards the boy trotted off to his room, played for a while, and came back later to suck on the pacifier for another hour. And that went on throughout the first day...

He spent the second day running back and forth between his room and the pacifier, sucking for a while and going back to play.

On day three he often looked out of his room to see if the pacifier was still hanging on the wall, though he spent much less time actually sucking on it.

Long story short, by the end of the week the boy had forgotten about the pacifier.

This story is already ten years old, and the pacifier is still stuck to that wall. Why? To remind the parents (and anyone else who stops by) that their children's needs should always be met in kind.

Children like this are quick to pick up subjects at school that require a lot of speaking, while the exact sciences tend to be a bit more difficult. After all, they think best while speaking and when other people are paying attention to them.

How do yellow-vectored people study for exams? They read a page and then head over to the kitchen. After eating half of what is in the refrigerator, they walk back to their book and read one more page before going to have a smoke. Then they read one more page, after which they chat for a little while on the phone. That entire cycle repeats itself over and over: kitchen, cigarette, tea, coffee, and phone. By the time evening rolls around, the refrigerator is empty, they are out of cigarettes, their phone is broken, and only a few pages have been read. The next morning they head to their exam, flunking if it is written. Remember that they absolutely have to speak if they want to think well (or at least whisper to themselves — articulating what they are thinking). Of course, that is when they hear someone tell them to close their mouth, at which point their thought process shuts down as well...

On the other hand, they do fine if it is an oral exam, since yellow-vectored people can talk well and for quite a while even on subjects they know nothing about.

Once a yellow-vectored student was about to take a zoology exam. She had spent her study time wandering between her phone and the refrigerator, though she had been able to memorize the information in the study guide about fleas. However, she was asked to talk about dogs, and so she answered, "Dogs are mammals with fur that can sometimes be home to fleas. So let's talk about the anatomy of the flea..." The teacher listened to her colorful story about those fleas before commenting, "That's all very interesting, but it isn't quite what you were asked to talk about." She drew another topic, this time about cats. Starting off with equal enthusiasm, she began, "Cats are mammals with fur that can sometimes be home to fleas. So let's talk about the physiology of the flea." After a repeat performance, the teacher returned, "Great, but again, that's not what you were asked! Try one more topic, and if you can get it right, I'll give you an A." The student drew again, coming up with fish... Scrunching it up in her hands, she said, "Fish do not have fur, but if they did, it might have fleas." And off she went...

Yellow-vectored children are fast learners when it comes to languages, and are especially good at speaking (brown-vectored students are the ones who have the grammar down pat). They are great at memorizing things so long as they have the chance to speak them out loud.

CHARACTER AND HABITS

Yellow-vectored people are extroverts and optimists. They are kind-hearted and generous, though careless and irresponsible (speak first; think later). They are easily appeased and do not hold grudges, though they are very capable of acting aggressively in the heat of the moment. Happily, that aggression is most often verbal.

A fantastic sense of humor is second nature to yellow-vectored people, who, when in their element, are like rays of sunshine warming those around them. They are the life of the party, great at having a good time, and simply happy, constantly upbeat people. You will never be disappointed by them unless you are expecting something productive (besides chit-chat or a great meal).

Once the mood turns sour, however, remember that yellow-vectored people are the first to panic. They will do anything to grab the attention of those around them, including making a mountain out of any molehill they can find. Listening to an emotional story complete with tragic expressions and frenzied gesticulation, you would be excused for thinking the world is about to end — happily, the only problem is that a few lightbulbs burnt out.

Their favorite color, of course, is yellow, and their favorite shape is the oval. Incidentally, yellow is the color of appetite, so feed your guests on a yellow tablecloth if you want them to really dig in. If you would rather they ate less, use a blue one (that is why orange-vectored people always have blue dishes and a blue tablecloth on hand for when guests show up). Note that normal restaurants are usually decorated in warm colors (yellow, orange, or brick red), while buffets prefer blue tones.

What do yellow-vectored people do when visiting friends? They eat, of course! And when they finish the first round, they ask for seconds, making it clear why orange-vectored people do not invite them over.

Yellow-vectored people are only able to work when they are a little bit hungry. On the one hand, they crash on the couch as soon as they eat their fill, happy as a lark, if incapable of getting anything done. An empty stomach, on the other hand, puts them in a foul mood, so productivity means finding the happy medium between hunger and satisfaction.

The two silliest questions a wife can ask her yellow-vectored husband when he gets home from work are, "Are you hungry?" and "How are you?" Most important is to stick a piece of meat in his mouth as soon as he walks in the door, after which he just wants to be told that his dinner is waiting in the kitchen.

Yellow-vectored people eat at a leisurely pace when nothing out of the ordinary is going on around them, content to savor each individual flavor. But just imagine what a person with a strong yellow vector and a strong orange vector would look like: a glutton who does his best to eat ahead of time as well...

I remember going to my first buffet when I was young. For a regular kid, it was unbelievable: you pay a small amount and eat as much as you want! I grabbed two trays right away, packing the first with soup, an entrée, and a dessert. The second was for soup (a different kind), an entrée (also a different kind), and juice. Across the mound of food I could barely see an ice cream cup with a cherry on top. "That has my name all over it," I thought.

When I got to the cashier with my trays and paid for the food, she looked at me as if wondering who else I was getting food for. I smiled spitefully and asked, "Is there a problem?" I polished off the first tray quickly, happy as a clam. The second was a bit harder: the soup was all right, but the second entrée pushed me over the edge. The juice's added weight did nothing to relieve the discomfort in my stomach, and I still had the cherry-topped ice cream ahead of me. I popped the cherry into my mouth and suddenly realized that if I swallowed it, the entire raging mass would come heaving back up. Of course, spitting it out would be terrible manners.

And so I sat there with the cherry in my mouth for quite a while before getting up and heading slowly for the door. I never did swallow that cherry — the danger refused to pass. But do you know what was most frustrating about the entire experience? By the next day I was back to being as hungry as ever!

What do yellow-vectored people do at night once everyone else in the house is asleep? They quietly ease their way over to the edge of the bed, get up, tiptoe to the refrigerator, and happily scarf down everything their orange-vectored wife kept from them during the day!

Yellow-vectored people are deliberate and easy-going when it comes to alcohol: taste and variety are much more important than alcohol content and quantity.

They have a hard time going for too long with nothing in their mouth — if they are not eating, drinking, or talking, they want to be chewing some gum or smoking. A typical yellow-vector problem is biting their tongue or cheeks as a result of eating, talking, and thinking, all at the same time... Their tongue is simply not capable of keeping up with everything going on.

Their handwriting is large and sprawling, with words that look especially like horizontal spirals (springs) when you look at them upside down. The fact that each word is big enough to fit on an entire page points to the lack of concern they have for saving paper (incidentally, red-vectored people cannot even fit one word on a page).

LOVE AND SEX

The yellow vector offers below-average sexual potential. Their favorite part of sex is the kissing, which they are happy to do over every inch of their partner's body. Yellow-vectored men love talking about sex and boasting about their conquests, though in reality they have little to brag about. Oral sex, on the other hand, is right up their alley; the problem is everything else.

Yellow-vector screams of passion released mid-orgasm can be heard by the next-door neighbors, not to mention the people in the next room. Stuffing a hand, pillow, or cat into their mouth to keep them quiet, however, can have an adverse effect on their health.

Two yellow-vectored people can live happily together if they can come to an agreement: "Today you listen to me, and tomorrow I'll listen to you" (although neither of them minds talking at the same time). They are otherwise perfectly compatible — who besides another yellow-vectored person knows how to feed them right? They are also great in the bedroom together, rarely reading past the 69 position in the *Kama Sutra*.

Yellow-vector fidelity is a fairly complicated issue. They have no particular drive to cheat on their partners, though their marital irresponsibility is no different from the rest of their lives.

HEALTH

In general the yellow vector is healthy: if they live happy lives with a delicious and varied diet, they should not have any serious health issues.

On the other hand, if their diet is not up to yellow-vector standards (quality- or variety-wise), their metabolism starts giving them problems (obesity, atherosclerosis, diabetes, and more).

The yellow vector covers the mouth and esophagus, but not the stomach. That is why gastritis and stomach ulcers come into play with a completely different vector (the blue one).

Herpes of the lips and stomatitis are typical problems for yellow-vectored people, as they stem from a vector-specific psychological cause. The same can be said of the chronic tonsillitis that comes from a stifled yellow vector.

Yellow-vectored people respond to stress first by trying to

eat the negativity away, generally with an excessive amount of sweets (bulimia[15]). If the stress intensifies or continues over a longer period of time, their eating behavior jumps into the opposite ditch (a sign of yellow-vector neurosis): they eat very little and care little about what they eat, sometimes refusing to eat altogether (anorexia[16]). Yellow-vector neurosis is also characterized by psychogenic mutism, dryness of the mouth, and nail biting.

While a balanced yellow vector makes for a "brightly colored balloon" that showers happiness on everyone nearby, neurosis makes for a "popped (or flat) balloon" lying motionless on the pavement.

Three things are needed to treat yellow-vector neurosis: tasty and varied food, patient listeners, and oral sex (in both directions).

Here is a quick story about neurosis. I have not been able to sing since I was a boy. The problem was not that I never learned; to be honest, I have never even tried (since I was seven) and therefore do not even really know what it is like. You have to get me pretty drunk if you want to hear me break something out.

This is all I know: in first grade something happened that I did not think was significant at the time, but that for some reason I remember to this day. We had a wonderful (probably) vocal teacher

---

[15] Bulimia ("ravenous hunger") is an eating disorder characterized by a suddenly strong appetite that comes in fits accompanied by an agonizing hunger.

[16] Anorexia is a condition marked by zero appetite and no hunger or a conscious decision not to eat.

— an older lady with a strong yellow vector that was coupled with an orange vector (like many teachers). Of course, that meant she pulled no punches: after one lesson she mentioned about me, "When that boy sings, it's the worst sound I've heard in my life." And that was the last time I tried singing...

CURSING

Yellow-vectored people have one more passion: they adore using obscenities. However, they differ from black-vectored people, who curse to fill up the spaces between words, in that they have an artistic way of using obscene language that could almost be called cultured. They are the kind of people who use bad language such that in a way it seems natural.

FILMS TO WATCH (WITH YELLOW-VECTORED CHARACTERS)

- Silence of the Lambs, directed by Jonathan Demme, USA, 1991 (Dr. Hannibal Lecter, played by Anthony Hopkins)
- Interview with the Vampire: The Vampire Chronicles, directed by Neil Jordan, USA, 1994 (almost all characters)

Visit my site www.psy8.net to enjoy the Vector Test, the Vector Gallery (pictures, movies and citations of all eight vectors), the article about the compatibility of vectors, answers to readers' questions, and more.

Chapter 7. The Green Vector — Eyes

Beauty Will Save the World

Some of us have had particularly sensitive eyes ever since we were born. In our system those people are accounted for in the green vector, one Viktor Tolkachev referred to as the "visual" vector.

You can take the Vector Test on my site www.psy8.net

So how can green-vectored people get pleasure from their significant area? Most of all they love gazing at beauty, or the harmony of colors and shapes. We can even take that one step further and say that beauty is to them as meat is to yellow-vectored people. Beautiful sights give their life joy, while a life bereft of them (something that happens all too often) forces green-vectored people to fill the void themselves: their lives turn into theaters where they play the lead role. Most important for this process is that people pay attention to them, which is why green-vectored people are constantly preoccupied with how they are perceived by others.

Compliments for them are more than a formality; they are the nutrients they (both men and women) need for survival. It is only when fed and watered by plentiful compliments that the green-vector "flower" can bloom. Women like this make a habit of getting to the office in the morning and spending the first chunk of their day incapable of working: they walk around, doing their best to chat with everyone in the office so as to pick up at least a few words from each person on how they look. They get to work once they have had their fill of compliments.

Mirrors are the focal point of green-vectored homes, hanging in the bathroom and kitchen as well as sitting on a shelf in the bedroom. Cars are also littered with them, though every last one is pointed at the driver. This vector has a tendency toward vanity that can sometimes be taken to the extreme of narcissism[17].

Green-vectored people are mostly helpless in everyday life: they have no idea what to do in tough situations, and so they need help and protection from the people around them. However, because their role is non-essential (they do not manage, build, or hunt for food), there is a chance they will simply be forgotten. That is why they feel the need to keep drawing attention to themselves, something that turns into *exhibitionism*.

Exhibitionism can be sexual (the kind of people who crawl out from behind bushes with their pants around their ankles), though most often it is non-sexual: any kind of self-demonstration or attempt to attract attention to one's self (models, actors, and the entire show business).

The reverse phenomenon — a passion for peeping (*voyeurism*) — is also linked to the green vector: some are content

---

[17] Narcissism is a character trait marked by an exclusive obsession with one's self. The term comes from a Greek myth about Narcissus, a good-looking young man who rejected the love of the nymph Echo. As punishment he was doomed to fall in love with his reflection in a lake and die of that love.

to spy through keyholes or the windows across the way, while others buy telescopes and keep track of their entire neighborhood.

Because green-vectored people are fairly helpless, they generally listen to the alpha (the authority in their life). This vector takes the back seat and is vulnerable to both suggestion and hypnotism.

Green-vectored people use a scale of beauty to judge everything in their lives, including non-visual sensations like beautiful aromas, ugly behavior, beautiful sounds, and so on. They are the ones who thought up the slogan, "beauty will save the world"[18].

They also attach excessive value to how things and events look. As a result, they sometimes fall prey to swindlers offering something worthless in a pretty package. The same is true for how green-vectored people see those around them: they are so trusting that they believe people who can turn a phrase — an experienced gypsy, for instance.

Green-vectored people try to decorate everything around them in their everyday lives, making it attractive and memorable. Quite a bit of what they have at home and at their job serves no greater purpose than as eye candy, while buying an expensive but beautiful trinket with the last of their savings betrays a lack of thought for baser needs like how they will buy food. That is why

---

[18] This phrase from *The Idiot*, by Dostoevsky, is generally understood to be taken literally, in contrast to the author's understanding of what beauty is. The book saw Dostoevsky diverge significantly from accepted views on aesthetics, writing instead about internal beauty, the beauty of the soul, and the sum of moral qualities that make up a "positively beautiful person."

trusting them with the family budget can be dangerous, leaving black- and yellow-vectored family members to die of hunger.

The cars driven by green-vectored people are just another thing for them to decorate: they repaint the body, fill the cabin with toys and pictures, and, of course, would never dream of tinting their windows (the people who do tint their car windows are black- and violet-vectored). How would anyone see all the beauty — including the driver — that lies within?

TEARS OF SADNESS AND JOY

The green vector is the most emotional of the eight vectors, given that tears are a way of activating its significant zone in lieu of other stimulations. Some green-vectored women love breaking into tears at the slightest provocation, making one up if they cannot find anything suitable. They might cry all night after seeing their man look at them askance, for instance.

Sometimes they get in so deep that they start thinking up ever more reasons to be upset. In the worst case scenario — green-vector neurosis — that sensitivity becomes their dominant psychological feature: they ferret out the implications of everything people say, even when those people have no idea what is going on. Mistrust then leads to regrettable misunderstandings in their lives.

Green-vectored people are extremely sensitive: they react strongly to everything they see and hear, crying at the theater and movies, when reading books, and when watching TV. They even think up sentimental endings to books and movies that also leave them in tears. Not only that, however, but they also adore imagining a tragic, if beautiful finale for the story of their lives.

Can you guess how green-vectored women watch horror movies? From around the corner or with their hands over their face.

"Have they killed him yet? I'm too scared to watch..." Meanwhile, the brown-vectored husband, who loves tormenting his wife, is also watching: "Yep, they killed him, you can watch." She crawls out from behind cover just when blood spurts everywhere: "A-a-a-ah! Why would you say that?!" She bursts into tears, and he comforts her. They make a great couple: he tormented her a bit and then calmed her down (double the happiness for the brown vector), while she cried and was soothed (double the happiness for the green vector).

People like this jump back and forth between sadness and happiness at the drop of a hat, victims of quickly changing moods.

Incidentally, green-vectored people are also prone to tears of happiness. And it is not only scenes from movies or incidents in their life that does it for them: some men can get teary-eyed just looking at the powerful beauty of nature.

Nature for the green vector is the height of beauty on earth (after their own reflection in the mirror), as its colors and shapes are flawless. Contemplating it gives green-vectored people balance, heals quite a few diseases, and gives their life particular flavor. However, the flip side is that green-vectored people living far from nature and without access to it can wilt like a dainty flower in the desert. Green-vectored people who grow up surrounded by nature and then move to the city can suffer from poor vision, especially if they live in drab new apartment blocks.

MIRACLES

Some green-vectored people believe in omens, others in horoscopes, and still more in fortune-telling. Regardless, they have one thing in common: they all live in expectation of a *miracle*. Their belief in *miracles* is even so selfless that they actually do happen in their lives! Most surprising is the fact that they do not have to do anything for those miracles to happen (red-vectored people are also lucky, though they have to work to get luck on their side).

Green-vectored people are imagination-driven dreamers with fantasies sometimes so strong that they are indistinguishable from real life. Their dreams can sometimes be like a TV show where each night they have a continuation of the previous night's installment. Green-vectored people are known for their *prophetic dreams* and other presentiments, including *clairvoyance*.

Their internal make-up is so fine-tuned that they can sense vibrations other people cannot. They get subtle signals from the information field about events in the future (or those occurring right now, but on the other side of the planet).

Green-vectored children especially can see things others — especially adults — cannot. If your child says he sees something that you do not, hold off on taking him to see a psychiatrist. They have a hard time thinking outside the box in situations like yours, preferring instead to refer to their "directory of disorders" that has something like this written in it (the language has been adapted): "If the child sees something the doctor does not see, the child is schizophrenic." And with that, thousands of ultrasensitive children are transformed into invalids to be treated by psychotropic drugs.

Many people actually saw "something unusual" when they were young, though they are careful to hide that for fear of the suspicious looks cast by those around them. More often than not, these phenomena disappear with childhood, though they sometimes do remain throughout adult life as extrasensory abilities.

This vector is also characterized by other fringe conditions that are poorly understood by modern science: déjà vu[19], sleepwalking[20], and day dreaming.

GREEN-VECTORED MEN

Green-vectored men are gentle, sensitive, and vulnerable, capable of deep sympathy and empathy. They are preoccupied with the way they look and love beautiful things, though without the brown vector that has nothing to do with homosexuality. It is just that the green vector (without a black, red, or orange vector to counterbalance it) makes men a bit feminine.

Can you imagine a young boy with this makeup being drafted into the army and trained to kill? He would get sick, die, or become nothing more than cannon fodder. The green vector is the most

---

[19] Déjà vu (from French, "already seen") is a psychological condition during which a person feels like they have already experienced a similar situation. However, they are generally not able to remember any details from the instance they think they are remembering.

[20] Sleepwalking (somnambulism) is an abnormal condition during which people do things in a dream state. Their behavior looks purposeful and reasoned, though they are actually acting in accordance with what they are currently dreaming.

delicate, meaning that survival in tough conditions (war, siege, or a deserted island) is doubtful at best.

Green-vectored men can do beautiful things for the sake of their beloved women. The red vector on its own is capable of those feats, though its heroism is primitive: a man might climb up water pipes to get to the woman he loves and ravish her right there. The green vector, on the other hand, might do something beautiful without a sense of resolve or purpose: a green-vectored man could stand for hours outside the window of the woman he loves holding a bouquet of flowers and have no idea what to do next. But the combination of red and green makes a man Prince Charming himself: he sets off fireworks, stands under the window holding flowers, and then, of course, climbs up the pipe to the fifth floor and...

Lastly, green-vector character couples with the *brown vector* and its heightened anal sensitivity to create fertile soil for homosexuality. While men with both green and brown vectors are not *necessarily* homosexual, note that both of them are strongly developed for practically everyone with that orientation.

INTELLECT AND IMPRACTICALITY

The green vector has been blessed genetically with strong intellectual potential. Green-vectored people have wide-reaching knowledge of a variety of areas, though, in contrast to their red-vectored friends, they rarely make great discoveries.

Green-vectored people have excellent visual memory, meaning they can see a picture and imprint it indelibly in their extensive "filing cabinet." They have a hard time remembering information that is spoken to them, as they need to see it with their own eyes. "A picture is worth a thousand words" is a phrase aimed directly at green-vectored people, while for blue-vectored people the opposite is true. Incidentally, black- and orange-vectored people need to touch things, as they trust neither their eyes nor their ears (people like that are referred to as *kinesthetic*).

The green vector is designed for fast and vivid right-brain thought that is completely lacking in logic. Children like this make great students and often win medals for their studies, though they have a hard time finding a practical use for their knowledge and talents.

The majority of them sit high above reality, which is why they need someone next to them who can take care of their needs and create the ideal conditions for their creative or intellectual work. That person could, for example, be a kind of producer who works to promote their talents and abilities.

If things turn out differently, green-vectored people risk becoming unrecognized geniuses who create only for themselves. Many people get a fantastic education and spend their whole lives with no one finding a need for them — they paint or come up with great ideas, though no one finds out until after they are dead. The problem here is not a native bashfulness; they are simply incapable of getting their life on track.

Green-vectored people are sometimes so impractical that they have a hard time applying their intellect to life's everyday situations. They might visit the bank, for instance, pick up a deposit slip, see all the numbers they have to enter correctly, and start to feel a little sick. On the other hand, they do always have a trick up their sleeves: they attract attention (for example, by starting to cry) and the people around them rush over to help. Blue-vectored people, incidentally, are even more impractical: they cannot even cry for show. Put them in a similar situation and they will probably leave the slip sitting right there and just go home...

LOVE AND SEX

The green vector only has a very low sexual potential (Viktor Tolkachev even claimed it had none whatsoever). Sex for many green-vectored people is an ugly, unnecessary process they are willing to do anything to avoid. Green-vectored women often discuss this problem with their psychologists. Rolling their eyes and sighing aloud, they tell their awful tale: "My husband is a sexual maniac! He wants to have sex twice a month!"

Women like that remain infantile in their relationships for their entire life: they love being beautifully wooed (flowers, chocolate, kissing their hands), fall in love with characters from books, and sometimes never even get married. Green-vectored girls mature late and prefer men who are older than they are (whose sex drive has already slowed significantly). Nature has made them more suitable for raising children than for making them.

For the same reason, green-vectored people are sometimes prone to agalmatophilia[21], or falling in love with works of art. After all, paintings and statues are sometimes absolutely gorgeous, and

---

[21] Agalmatophilia is a kind of fetish where the subject gets satisfaction from owning an image of the human body (paintings, statues, or pictures). The term comes from the Greek words for statue and love.

they have no need for sex — what more could a green-vectored person want besides just gazing at and enjoying them? The same is true of erotic films: green-vectored people are perfectly happy when the scene following beautiful foreplay shows two people sleeping soundly in each other's arms.

Green-vectored people prefer tender kisses on the eyes to all other forms of sexual attention. They also might mount a mirror on their bedroom ceiling to be aroused by looking at their own naked body. If they do in fact have sexual potential (thanks to other vectors), they can get very turned on by looking at erotica, and even cry during orgasms. It may not be difficult to imagine an emotional woman accompanying sex with tears of happiness, though a man sobbing during an orgasm is perhaps more out of the ordinary...

Many women dream of finding a gentle man — in other words, a green-vectored one. Men like that also look for beautiful, vivacious, and well-groomed women (read: green-vectored ones). Two green-vectored people make a fantastic pair: they hardly need either food or sex. All they need for happiness is to stare at each other or nature.

The love shown by the green vector is enthusiastic and demonstrative, if not as deep as it might seem. Green-vectored people fall deeply in love, and then...fall in love again — after all, life is boring without the passion of infatuation!

Recall Romeo in the first lines of Shakespeare's eponymous tragedy as he rapturously discusses his love:

I am too sore enpierced by his [Cupid's] shaft

To soar with his light feathers, and so bound,

I cannot bound a pitch above dull woe:

Under love's heavy burden do I sink.

So who does Romeo feel so strongly about? Juliet? No! His fiery speech is inspired by Rosaline! At first he did not even want to go to the ball (where he would later meet Juliet) to avoid being tormented by memories of Rosaline:

What doth her beauty serve, but as a note

Where I may read who pass'd that passing fair?

However, his friends convince him to go to the ball, where he sees Juliet and makes a complete switch:

Did my heart love till now? forswear it, sight!

For I ne'er saw true beauty till this night.

And farther on:

With Rosaline, my ghostly father? no;

I have forgot that name, and that name's woe.

Green-vectored people can go into an unusual trance their cynical red-vectored friends would call "sexual excitement." The following story from a seminar participant graphically demonstrates both the green-vector pull toward nature as well as the way green-vectored people talk:

"When I was 18 I happened across a magical winter forest. The snow-draped trees sparkled in the rays of the setting sun, while the softness enchanted so deeply that I was afraid to move a muscle. At that moment I felt a complete oneness with nature I had never before experienced. It was a state of exquisite closeness and intimacy that many yearn for in the arms of their beloved, though find only rarely

and only to have flash by. Enveloped in a growing sexual excitement, I released my body into the greedy embrace of nature itself. And that is when I was blown away by one of the most unusual orgasms of my life..."

APPEARANCE AND HABITS

Recognizing green-vectored people is never all that difficult, as their attractive, put-together appearance makes them stand out in a crowd. Whether they stay up to date on the latest whims of fashion or simply develop their own style, the way they look is impressive. The brown-vector is also known for its neat clothes, though that neatness stems from a tendency more toward tidiness than beauty. Green-vectored people, on the other hand, could make even a mess look good.

Green-vectored people are generally slender. Their faces, of course, are highlighted by eyes that may be large, unusually shaped, or unusually colored — in short, they are prominent. Contacts or glasses are frequent accessories necessitated by a modern life that is hard on highly sensitive eyes.

Green-vectored women (and men as well) often look younger than they are and love wearing jewelry: rings all over their fingers, bracelets, and large hooped earrings. They also are big fans of the many accessories they can use to decorate their clothes and personal belongings, and prefer happily colored clothes — all the many shades of green, especially. Of course, piercings and tattoos are also par for the green-vector course, though only if they also have a strong orange vector.

People with an unaccepted green vector may dress brightly

(even to a glaring degree), though without taste or style. They certainly attract attention from people around them (just like any bright object), though that attention is lost just a second later.

Green-vectored people are thrown into a panic over even the smallest stain on their clothes, and would never wear other people's clothes. While thrift stores are heaven for the orange vector, the green vector would not dream of wearing something someone else has worn. Just imagine the tragedy a green-vectored child born into a big orange-vectored family would live through (green-vector neurosis would probably be in the cards for that child).

Obviously, their favorite color is green, and their favorite shape is the circle. That is why they are drawn throughout their lives to round and green things: round tables, round chairs, and round picture frames for rectangular pictures. They adore freshly cut flowers and everything else they can use to decorate their home.

There is one more shape besides the circle that green-vectored people find delightful: the golden ratio[22]. The golden ratio is considered to be a natural geometric law, which is why the green-vector eye finds it so pleasant. There are many things in nature, including parts of the human body, that reflect the golden ratio. Leonardo da Vinci's famous painting of a man with his arms and legs

---

[22] The golden ratio (divine proportion) is when the ratio of two quantities is the same as the ratio of their sum to the larger of the two quantities. In other words, we can cut a square off of a rectangle with the golden ratio and get a new, smaller rectangle with the exact same ratio between its long and short sides. The ratio of the long side to the short side is 1.618, while the ratio of the short side to the long side is 0.618.

outspread along a circle is dedicated to this relationship.

Green-vector handwriting is beautiful and refined, like how the best girls at school write: letters are rounded, capital letters have curlicues or other decorations, and signatures are works of art. Both children and adults prefer to write using colored ink (green, most often), and enjoy doodling wherever they can find some free space.

Green-vectored people speak brightly, emotionally, and even theatrically, with an abundance of facial expressions and gestures.

They have great memories and can go back and relive anything that happened in their life by finding any old trinket that reminds them of it. "Ah, my husband gave me this 20 year ago," triggers stories, tears, and bittersweet memories.

Many green-vectored people have such cold biochemistry that they even have a hard time keeping warm in the summer — their hands, feet, and ears are always cold... However, that biochemistry keeps them looking young all the way into old age: they retain some element of childishness (and sometimes infantilism) throughout their lives.

Green-vectored people are nibblers for whom the beauty and harmony of their food is most important: the spoonful of oatmeal they have for dinner is served on a spotlessly white tablecloth and accompanied by two fancy spoons next to three equally fancy forks. If the table is set carelessly, they may lose their appetite entirely; it was actually green-vectored people who got together with orange-vectored people to invent etiquette and good behavior. The former cannot do without beauty, and the latter have to have rules.

When it comes to alcohol, green-vectored people are lightweights. They attract even more attention when drunk, sometimes even stripping off their clothes in public. Because alcohol is too strong a substance for them, they prefer smoking a little light marijuana — many famous artists have used it to stimulate their imagination.

Regardless of their love of nature, green-vectored people do not like hiking. Instead, they enjoy nature surrounded by the comfort of warmth and cleanliness, far away from any mosquitos.

PROFESSIONS AND WORK

It goes without saying that green-vectored people are first and foremost actors. However, there are not enough jobs for them all, so the rest often set up theaters in their own lives (at home or at work).

They are talented artists, sculptors (if they have a black vector), photographers, designers, modellers, stylists, makeup artists, barbers, museum attendants, tour guides (if they have a yellow vector), and cameramen.

Green-vectored doctors give excellent, accurate diagnoses, as they can see diseases by their micro-symptoms. They are generally ophthalmologists, radiologists, diagnosticians, or nurses ("sister of mercy" is perfect for the green-vector character).

Green-vectored people also make excellent teachers at schools and kindergartens: they get along well with children, though they can sometimes get pushed around.

Fast thought processes and being in-tune with other people's emotions lets them work with in client-facing positions, especially where tact and attention are needed. However, it is important to remember that green-vectored people are volatile in an aggressive environment, prone to bursting into tears and running away.

Experienced bosses know there are other ways to incentivize their green-vectored employees besides money. Beautiful compliments, especially those said in public, are much more important than any kind of monetary bonus. Imagine what a find those employees are for stingy orange-vectored bosses!

KINDNESS WILL SAVE THE WORLD

Out of all the eight vectors, green-vectored people are the kindest. They are philanthropic, hospitable, tactful, and friendly, and they never forget anyone's birthday. Other people's attitudes, opinions, and health are always given close attention.

Green-vectored people can empathize with and make sense of other people's emotions as if they were their own, and their kindness makes them great shoulders to cry on. After all, complaining about life always feels better when you are with someone who can really sympathize with you.

Even going beyond that, people like this subconsciously assume the lives of others. When a friend comes to complain about how she is having a fight with her husband, she is having issues at work, and her leg is bothering her, the next day the green-vectored woman's leg also starts to give her trouble and parallel problems start to appear at home and at the workplace. Sometimes green-vectored people immerse themselves so fully in other people's lives that they have a hard time returning to their own — one they take relatively little responsibility for. Some spend years playing a character and experiencing their friends' feelings.

If they have a role model, they may adopt his posture, gestures, habits, and way of speaking (all the while having no idea that a transformation is taking place).

These qualities are beautifully illustrated in Woody Allen's film Zelig, where the main character subconsciously transforms into the people he talks with.

THE FINER POINTS OF COMMUNICATION

The green vector prefers physically talking from a distance: in comparison with the general norm for personal space, they take another half step away from the person they are speaking with. Of course, that makes it hard for them to have conversations with black-vectored (and sometimes orange-vectored) people, as they are prone to invading that personal space.

Green-vectored people attach strong value to looking the other person in the eye when they are talking. Getting into a staring match, on the other hand, is just as unpleasant as the opposite problem, and the discomfort generally makes them avoid eye contact altogether.

People like this have no tolerance for rudeness, vulgarity, toilet humor, or obscene language, all of which throws them for a loop or makes them cry.

One way to manipulate green-vectored people is by playing to their soft spot. If they believe and sympathize with a clever manipulator, they will do anything they can to help.

ON ANIMALS

Green-vectored people could never squish a worm, chicks who have fallen out of their nest reduce them to tears, and they will spend any amount of time to save a fly who fell into some milk. If your child has a strong green vector, you can be sure you will be opening a shelter for homeless animals or a veterinary hospital. All the suffering animals in your neighborhood will end up under your roof: "Mom, dad, this kitten will live with us too!"

Once during a seminar one of the women went for a walk during a break and returned in tears: "In the courtyard... there is... a hurt pigeon! A cat could just eat it! We have to do something!"

The group immediately splintered along vector lines. The teary green-vectored girls begged everyone else to save the pigeon, though they were unwilling to do anything themselves. The brown-vectored people said, "Does anyone have a needle and thread? We should sew up the wound..." The black-vectored participants had a simple solution: "We should just put it out of its misery." Yellow-vectored people said, "Pigeons taste terrible, so we're not going anywhere. Let's just chat here for a while." The orange-vectored group was as logical as ever: "Sure, a cat will eat the pigeon, a dog will eat the cat, the dog will be made into sausage, and we'll eat the dog. It's the circle of life." There were no red-vectored people that day, so there was no one to take charge. In the end, you can guess what happened: the pigeon was left on its own and the girl sat there crying for the rest of the lesson...

FAREWELL, SWEET WORLD!

As you are already aware, green-vectored people will do anything for attention. If their normal methods are not working, they may decide to try a "show suicide." Ultimately, they have no desire to take their own lives, as they are too concerned with the problem of how they will look in the coffin. Poisoning would leave them jaundiced, hanging would leave them blue in the face, and slitting a vein would leave them pale with blood all over them. Just thinking about how they would look after drowning or jumping from a rooftop makes them queasy.

Much better to throw pills around their apartment and write everyone a letter beforehand: "On such-and-such a day at such-and-such a time I will leave this world, so the door will be open." Then they hang themselves using a thin cord or jump from a first floor window (the second floor works if the first did not do the trick). Of course, disaster can also strike: green-vectored people occasionally take their act too far, climb onto the windowsill, slip, and fall in the wrong direction...

GREEN-VECTORED CHILDREN

Children with this vector need to be surrounded by pleasing shapes and colors. They also need to feel constantly protected: green-vectored babies should not spend more than 24 hours away from their mothers. They love going to sleep while it is still light outside, so long as someone else is nearby, and they need love, care, and shelter more and longer than other vectors.

Green-vectored boys are just as sensitive and gentle as

green-vectored girls, as tears are their first reaction to the problems life throws up in their path. Even the littlest things will have them sobbing, which is when their (black- and orange-vectored) mother comes over: "What are you howling there like a girl for? Stop it! Suck it up, you wimp! You're going to be a soldier, a pilot, a bodyguard, a protector, maybe a firefighter... Get out of here if you're going to be such a crybaby! Men don't cry!" Incidentally, that phrase — "men don't cry" — puts many boys on the path to green-vector neurosis.

Green-vectored boys generally hang around women: their mother, sister, or grandmother, for example. They prefer sitting at home sewing to taking apart a carburetor with their father.

Green-vectored children can lay on the couch doing nothing for hours. Their parents may think they are just lazy, but the truth is they are deep inside their rich imagination. The only thing the parents should do is give them paints or a pen — but never teach them how to draw! While they may never be great artists, they will be balanced people capable of expressing themselves on paper.

Children like this generally eat slowly and very little; it is almost as if they only need food for their eyes. They should never be made to eat, as that could ruin their metabolism and lead to any number of illnesses.

And what usually happens at kindergarten? The yellow- and black-vectored teacher says, "Kids, first you finish eating, then you can go play." Meanwhile, there is a round-eyed and green-vectored girl sitting there wondering where she will put all her food... Well, the soup she can leave on the floor — the cat has been eyeing it for a while. Her yellow-vectored friend would be happy to take her meat off her hands. She can wrap her noodles up in a napkin and throw them away later, but she'll go ahead and drink her juice herself. That juice is a complete lunch for the green vector, something that is perfectly natural — it is just how their organism is set up.

A MONKEY TALE

Viktor Tolkachev used to say that the main role for green-vectored monkeys in the troop is as day watchmen. They sit high up on a hill and use their excellent vision to see everything around them, including a leopard closing in on the troop. What happens next? The green-vectored monkeys let the yellow-vectored monkeys know about the threat, and they in turn loudly shout to warn the troop. That is when the red-vectored monkeys get involved, organizing their black-vectored members to gather up the troop's supplies and get ready to run. The red-vectored monkeys are assisted by the orange-vectored monkeys, who keep everyone disciplined and in line. The brown-vectored monkeys are last, gathering up everything that is left or was dropped in the rush, and with that the troops takes off to get away from the leopard. But what about the green-vectored watchman? He stayed there and everyone forgot about him, seeing as how the green vector is so numerous (there will always be a replacement). However, if the green-vectored watchman also has an orange vector, *and neither vector is accepted*, then the herd runs off and even shoves him toward the leopard (everyone else gets away while the hungry leopard eats his fill). Combining imbalanced green and orange vectors results in a *"sacrificial lamb"* (martyr complex[23]).

---

[23] A martyr complex is when a person has a propensity for suffering.

By the way, that combination of green and orange is a common one among women, though there is no sacrifice involved when both are accepted. To the contrary, it can be highly productive.

HEALTH

Just as with the other upper[24] vectors, the green vector is less than hardy: green-vectored people have weak immune systems, often catch colds, and so on. They — and especially men — enjoy getting sick, as they can lay on the couch with a tragic expression on their face: "This is it... I have a fever... [98.7] I'm dying..." Of course, what they really want is for everyone to jump in and take care of them, in which case they will be feeling fine by the next day. If, on the other hand, they do not get that attention (or if they just so desire!), they may stay sick for weeks.

Of course, all eye diseases are rooted in an imbalanced green vector. If green-vectored children witness violence or worse at home, a psychological shortsightedness or even partial blindness may quickly develop: "What's the point of seeing this world if it's so ugly?!"

When green-vectored people are in neurosis, they stop caring about their appearance, how they dress, what they create,

---

They see no other way to gain the love and attention of those around them in everyday life than by selflessly caring for them (stemming from a feeling of guilt), though at the same time they blame those people for their victimhood.

[24] The upper vectors are the ones above the mouth (green, blue, and violet), in contrast to the lower ones (black, red, orange, and brown). The yellow vector takes up the area between the two groups.

and even their dreams. They no longer notice the beauty around them, instead constantly taking offence and crying. The good news is that all it takes to quickly get them out of their neurosis is some attention, affection, and skillful compliments. The best medicine for green-vectored people is contemplating nature, beautiful paintings, and the harmonious things around them.

I would like to finish this chapter by talking about a problem some green-vectored people begin to deal with even in childhood. In science it is called body dysmorphic disorder, or a dissatisfaction with one's own body in laymen's terms. Something about their appearance seems ugly to them: their nose (or ears or mouth) is too big or too small, or their chest is not how they would like it to look. These are the people who visit plastic surgeons, though they are rarely able to find what they are looking for so long as deep down they still think of themselves as unattractive[25].

Because of this it is important to tell green-vectored children when they are very young that they are beautiful, and that there is no standard of beauty they have to meet.

Coupling the green and orange vectors can lead to a comical way of caring about one's appearance:

A woman visits a plastic surgeon and asks for breast implants.

"Ok," says the surgeon, "the latest silicone implant costs $5000."

"No," the woman answers, "that's too much."

"All right, then the next best option costs $2000: the material

---

[25] Michael Jackson went through an incredible number of surgeries, though he was never able to come to terms with his appearance before his death.

isn't quite as good, though in general it will do the job just as well."

"That's still too pricey for me," the woman continues, "Do you have anything cheaper?"

"Well, let's do this then: I'll make incisions in your armpits, and all you'll have to do whenever you want your breasts to expand is flap your arms and pump them full of air. That will cost $200."

"Oh, that sounds great!"

The operation is successful, and a few weeks later the woman is at a restaurant and has her eye on a man at the bar. She flaps her arms like she was taught, her breasts expand, and... The man gets up, walks over, and starts energetically stamping his feet, saying, "Madam, it looks like we have the same doctor!"

FILMS TO WATCH (WITH GREEN-VECTORED CHARACTERS)

- Amélie, directed by Jean-Pierre Jeunet, France and Germany, 2001 (Amélie, played by Audrey Tautou)

- Some Like It Hot, directed by Billy Wilder, USA, 1959 (Sugar Kane Kowalczyk, played by Marilyn Monroe)

- Zelig, directed by Woody Allen, USA, 1983 (Leonard Zelig, played by Woody Allen)

Visit my site www.psy8.net to enjoy the Vector Test, the Vector Gallery (pictures, movies and citations of all eight vectors), the article about the compatibility of vectors, answers to readers' questions, and more.

CHAPTER 8. THE BLUE VECTOR — EARS

LIVING IN SILENCE

As we get ready to go to bed in the evening, our bodies produce special chemicals that help us go to sleep (one of them, *melatonin*, is referred to as the "sleep hormone"). Then in the morning we produce hormones that wake us up (*cortisol* and others). However, that is not true of everyone...

Some of us have been blessed with a surprising singularity: that process is reversed! As soon as the sun drops below the horizon, people like this start producing hormones that get them feeling more active. These night owls have especially sensitive ears, and in our system belong to the blue vector.

You can take the Vector Test on my site www.psy8.net

Viktor Tolkachev called this the "aural" vector and thought that in primitive communities particularly keen hearing made blue-vectored people perfect night watchmen. Moreover, that responsibility required absolute silence, as even one's own body can interfere with all the noises it produces (beating heart, raspy breathing, growling stomach, and so on). That is why blue-vectored people have incredibly cold biochemistry: their heartbeat is barely audible, their breathing is shallow, and they do not snort, slurp, pass gas, or make any other bodily noises. They are "frozen" people...

While green-vectored people are exhibitionists (they want everyone to notice them), blue-vectored people could be called "inhibitionists": they do not want anyone to notice, distract, or pull them away without a very good reason.

Blue-vectored people constantly suppress their emotions in an attempt to prevent any unnecessary noises from popping out. After all, each emotion has a certain sound profile: the heart beats harder, breathing comes faster, and the stomach growls with more authority. With that said, blue-vectored people have emotions that are just as strong as those of green-vectored people, who you may remember are the most emotional of all the eight vectors. Blue-vectored people, however, do so much to suppress them that their emotional constitution is more "silent hysterics"...

Since people like this do not sleep at night, their bodies start producing sleep hormones in the morning when the sun comes up. As a result, morning and the beginning of each day is the time blue-vectored people want to sleep — just when our society requires them to be active. That is why they are drowsy at work or at school in the morning. Sometimes they even fall asleep at the wheel with tragic consequences. You have probably heard of famous musicians gifted with perfect pitch (and therefore a strong blue vector) whose lives came to an awful end during their morning commute.

INTELLECT AND MEMORY

In contrast to vision, which we can only use after we are born, our hearing gets to work much earlier. After about five months in the womb, babies begin taking in sound from the world around them via the mother's stomach.

By the way, blue-vectored children are different even in utero, as they are absolutely calm. They lie there practically motionless, something that often worries their sensitive mothers. In ultrasounds they can often be seen covering their tender ears as if to keep out what is already a noisy world — boom, boom, boom. That kind of baby may very well be born with damaged hearing.

Several years ago an unbelievable report about research done by English scientists circled the internet. Three hundred pregnant mothers began reading aloud a single fairy tale once they hit the six month mark. After their children were born, the scientists asked them to forget that story and never read it again. Imagine the researchers' surprise when many of the children were able to continue that fairy tale from any point in the story at three years of age!

Yes, that fact has already been proven: our brain is capable of perceiving, storing, and even somehow processing the audio information we receive long before birth. The idea of teaching children in the womb, it turns out, is not so harebrained after all. Of course, children may not be able to learn foreign languages before they are born, though knowledge will be well-received in the future.

In contrast to other vectors, blue-vector children are born with some knowledge already accumulated. They are also genetically predisposed to developing a strong intellect: blue-vectored people with the opportunity to reach their potential are the most intellectual of all the eight vectors (even ahead of the green vector). However, their intelligence is geared more toward working with large sets of data (analysis or synthesis) rather than generating great ideas.

Blue-vectored people also have a great memory: what they hear sticks with them straight through to the end of their lives. On the other hand, their memory is unique in that it is similar to a tape recorder. They learn a new piece of information, "record it to a cassette" (in short-term memory), and then pull out the cassette and put it on a shelf (in long-term memory). Because of that, if someone were to ask them out of the blue what five times four is, their first reaction would be confusion. To go back to our example, they are finding the right shelf, pulling out the cassette, sticking it into the tape player, fast-forwarding to the spot they are looking for, and pressing play. The answer will always be correct, even if looking for it takes some time.

But what happens at your normal, run-of-the-mill school? "Johnny!" the teacher yells to get his attention. "Five times nine??" "Uhh..." "What do you mean, 'uhh'?? You should know the answer in your sleep." Of course, there is no need for that, since Johnny does not sleep at night anyway; recalling the answer (especially in the morning) just takes some time.

It often turns out that these same intellectually superior children walk away from school with poor report cards. However, once we consider that blue-vectored men often have a black vector as well, the only place blue-vectored boys have to really be themselves at school is the gym. That is why many athletes, regardless of their typical black-vector appearance, have an untapped intellectual potential that comes from their suppressed blue vector.

When chatting with blue-vectored people, give them as much time as they need instead of demanding an answer right away. They are slow to begin new processes and equally slow to switch between different processes, giving them something in common with the brown vector. Productivity requires being comfortable psychologically (with no one pushing or pulling them) and, what is just as important, complete silence. Sadly, that is a rare occurrence indeed.

A blue-vectored boy gets home after a long, noisy day at school and needs some time to balance himself. He puts on his headphones, turns on his favorite music, and drifts away... But that is when his mother (with the loud squawk of a yellow- and orange-vector voice) comes in: "Peter!!! Did you take out the trash???!!!" So much for any kind of balance... But what can he do? He takes out the trash, sits back down, puts on his headphones, and goes back to his happy place... He only just has time to relax, however, when his grandmother barges in: "Sweetie! Have a pastry!" He could not care less about the pastry, as he could go for days without eating, but there is no sense insulting his grandmother. He eats it, puts on his headphones, and tries to quiet the storm gathering inside him. But the finishing touch is when his (brown-vectored) father walks in: "Son, let's go fix the toilet." ENOUGH... The boy can no longer live in a family that cannot give him a moment's peace and quiet. And that is why blue-vectored children (especially ones with a red vector to boot) run away from home relatively often.

Blue-vectored children do not put on their headphones to ignore you; they just need some time to recover psychologically. Regardless of their calm outward demeanor, they may have a hurricane raging inside them.

SOUNDS FROM HEAVEN

Normal people hear sounds in the 20Hz to 20kHz range. Blue-vectored people, on the other hand, use their extra-sensitive ears to hear even beyond that. They can perceive ultrasound[26] somewhat, but, most importantly, they can "hear" infrasound[27] — the same tool used by whales to send information thousands of miles from one end of the ocean to the other. Because of that, blue-vectored people sitting in New York can hear the "noise" made by hurricanes in the Pacific. They are incredibly weather-sensitive, having a presentiment of meteorological changes and many other natural events long before they ever happen.

Of course, hurricanes are not the only noise-makers at the infrasound level... Yes, it is true that some people are able to receive signals bouncing around planet Earth, and those people are blue-vectored. While green-vectored people are characterized by clairvoyance, their blue-vectored friends have clairaudience. The former receive information out of nowhere in picture form (snapshots, slides, or short video fragments); the latter hear it as

---

[26] Ultrasound is an oscillating sound wave with a frequency beyond the range that the normal human ear can hear (more than 20kHz). It occurs in nature as an element of natural sounds (wind, waterfalls, rain, pebbles skipping over water, and so on) as well as in the animal world.

[27] Infrasound is waves similar to audible ones, though they occur at frequencies lower than those the normal human ear can hear. The environment has little effect on infrasound, so it can travel long distances from the source. In nature it occurs during earthquakes, storms, hurricanes, and tsunamis, while it is also produced by powerful equipment like drilling tools, boilers, vehicles, and ventilation shafts.

voices. But how does our society treat people who hear "voices"? Even worse than it treats those who see "shadows." We even have a relevant joke: what is the difference between faith and schizophrenia? The first is when you talk to God; the second is when God answers.

Some children really can hear things that their peers and even adults cannot. However, psychiatrists, as you may remember, have a "directory of disorders" that talks about blue-vectored people similarly to how it talks about green-vectored ones (the language has been adapted): "If the child hears something the doctor cannot, the child is schizophrenic."

Ultimately, psychological health has nothing to do with whether people hear or see things others cannot; the most important criteria of "normalcy" are whether people can draw a line between our "general reality" and their own, and if they can adapt to normal life.

APPEARANCE AND OTHER FEATURES

Blue-vector ears always stand out in a crowd: they may be oversized, stick out, or be unusually shaped. However, they are often hidden behind long hair that both protect the sensitive organs and provide a gentle stimulation for the erogenous zone. Hair also serves to filter out all the unpleasantly high frequencies, resulting in a more harmonious sound.

Blue-vectored people are generally slender, and sometimes even frail. Their deeply set eyes and half-closed eyelids help them narrow the stream of visual information they receive and focus on what they can hear.

Their movements are very smooth, their body somewhat limp, their posture slumped (it looks like they have a rubber spine), and their body language and gestures minimal.

Just like the other upper[28] vectors, blue-vectored people prefer talking from a greater distance, taking an extra half-step away from the person they are talking with and also turning to face them at an angle that puts their dominant ear forward. Their hands are most often cold, while their handshake is weak (like a dead fish).

Blue-vectored people dress plainly, preferring dark (gray and blue) tones. Once in a while, however, they do dress stylishly and elegantly (though never loudly).

They speak softly and slowly, with a voice that is similar to a quiet brook — sometimes they even put those around them to sleep (or hypnotize them).

While blue-vectored people may look off to the side or right through you when listening, they have not lost interest. They also periodically nod their heads, something that is mistakenly taken to signify agreement. It actually is just a signal to let you know they are still listening.

This can often lead to funny situations in stores. An eloquent yellow-vectored salesman might be chatting with a blue-vectored client, beautifully describing all the different advantages a particular product offers while the client stands and silently nods her head. The

---

[28] The upper vectors are considered to be those with orifices above the mouth (green, blue, and violet), as opposed to the lower ones (black, red, orange, and brown). The yellow vector takes up the space between them.

salesman, elated by that "agreement," invites the client over to the cash register only to be declined respectfully. "Wait, what? But didn't you agree with everything I just said?!" "I only nodded because I was listening to you..."

Many blue-vectored people are left-handed, and an overwhelming majority of left-handed people have a strong blue vector.

Blue-vector handwriting is fairly original, with letters that are elongated (sometimes looking like a treble clef) and often slanted backwards.

Blue-vectored people cannot handle alcohol well and are usually indifferent to cigarettes.

Their favorite colors are different shades of blue, while their favorite shape is the hourglass.

LOVE AND SEX

The blue vector has even less sexual potential than the green one (the lowest out of all the vectors: almost none whatsoever). Their love is platonic[29], though, in contrast with their green-vectored friends, blue-vectored people experience emotions more deeply than the other vectors. Granted, nobody around them has any idea that that is true; instead they sit silently as their partners begin to doubt their love. "Do you love me?" "Yes." And that wraps

---

[29] Platonic love is a sublime feeling built on spiritual attraction without a sexual element. The term is derived from Plato (427—348 BCE), an ancient Greek philosopher who used the *Symposium* to discuss this kind of love with a person named Pausanias. He understood it to be the "ideal" love and one that is purely spiritual.

up the conversation.

While green-vectored people are turned on by erotic scenes, blue-vectored people are turned on by erotic (not sexual!) sounds like light breathing — you can forget mid-orgasmic yellow-vector screams. They love being gently kissed on the ear, while there is nothing that caresses their sensitive area like words of love from their partners.

Two blue-vectored people can live in complete harmony, needing neither food nor sex. They listen to their favorite music in two-person headphones and talk about the love they have for each other without ever opening their mouths, almost like fish...

Blue-vectored people also get along fairly well with green-vectored partners, as neither needs much food or sex and there are no strong cultural or intellectual differences between them. A pair like this does, however, have one problem: the blue-vectored partner spends each day in silence, while the green-vectored partner needs constantly changing emotions — first beautifully taking offence and then beautifully breaking into tears.

I know a blue- and green-vectored couple that has dealt with that difference in their characters for many years. The husband is a blue-vectored programmer, while his wife is a green-vectored designer. He sits there all day long tapping away at his computer, and she tells him long, emotional stories. Once she does not get a response, she cries, "You aren't listening to me at all!" Instantly turning away from the keyboard he answers, "Yes, I am." "Well, what did I just say?" This." And before that?!" "This." A bit more haughtily, "And before that...?" "This." And now horrified, "And what was before that...?" "This." He heard everything and recorded it on his "cassette tapes," letting him play it back whenever he needs to. However, that does not mean he got involved in the topic or shared the experience with his wife.

HEALTH

Blue-vectored people have fairly fragile health: they catch colds easily and can take a long time to recover even from light sicknesses. If their vector is not accepted, they can also suffer from chronic otitis (inflammation of the inner ear).

The main problem blue-vectored adults face is a lack of an emotional release. Their emotions are just as strong as those of green-vectored people, though there is no way for them to bubble out onto the surface. As a result, their most vulnerable organ is their stomach[30]: first they develop gastritis, then they move on to ulcers, and later they experience even worse problems. Because women generally find it easier to express their emotions regardless of their vector, men go through these problems much more often.

Once a 15-year-old boy suffering from a stomach ulcer visited a psychologist. He was young for that kind of problem, but there was no arguing with the facts... The boy was 100% blue-vectored: he was slender and had deeply set blue eyes, slightly narrowed eyelids, and ears that stuck out. During the hour-long meeting, however, they could not find a single cause for the problem: the boy's life had everything needed for a balanced blue vector. The situation only became clear when his mother walked into the office: she talked (or rather shouted) in such a shrill voice that the case was closed. And

---

[30] As strange as this may seem, stomach problems are related to the blue-vector rather than the yellow one!

what did the psychologist recommend? The approach was twofold: first, the mother took a voice correction course (fairly common these days), and second, the boy went through some psychological treatment. In three weeks the ulcer was gone.

I am not here to say that all ulcers can be treated by a pleasant voice or good music. On the other hand, how many doctors do you know who look at their patients' acoustic surroundings?

Blue-vector neurosis (besides causing deteriorated hearing and stomach problems) intensifies the helplessness prevalent in everyday life. Intellectual capacity and creative potential both drop noticeably.

What is the best way to treat blue-vectored people? Obviously, using their favorite music and the harmonious sounds of nature: the surf, rustling leaves, and babbling brooks. On the other hand, if you ask a few blue-vectored people what the most beautiful sound in the world is, they will whisper in unison: "silence..."

PROFESSIONS AND WORK

Their powerful intellect lets them work in a wide variety of fields requiring smarts and knowledge, while their excellent hearing opens the door for them to work as musicians and poets. Having a blue vector does not guarantee an unusual musical talent, though everyone with an ear for music is without a doubt blue-vectored. Blue-vectored people can also use their outstanding aural memory to study language — many of them go on to become excellent polyglots.

The blue vector needs complete peace and quiet with no distractions if it wants to get work done. The ideal option is a computer, which is why many programmers and system administrators fit the description of this vector.

On the other hand, blue-vectored people are absolutely worthless when it comes to working with their hands (except when it comes to keyboards and musical instruments).

It is important to note that the blue vector is the only one not motivated by money. Creating the right conditions for blue-vectored people and promoting their intellectual or creative product lets them put together fantastic projects worth fabulous sums, though they are unable to promote themselves. They would wither away without a producer nearby regardless of their talent and abilities.

In stark contrast to the red vector, blue-vectored people do not fight for power or external freedom; they are above many human passions and understand the futility of material achievements. Internal freedom, which no one can take away, and which does not depend on external circumstances or other people, is much more important to them.

CONVERSATION

Blue-vectored people are classic melancholies. Shy, timid, quiet, reserved, compliant, and delicate, their natural bashfulness eliminates practically all the desire they might have for career status or belongings. They are kind and wise, treating the people around them with understanding and grace. However, in everyday life they are even less practical and adapted than green-vectored people. In tough situations green-vectored people can attract attention and call for help by bursting into tears; blue-vectored people are incapable of expressing their feelings and emotions, so nobody knows how much they actually need help and support.

The blue vector is one of the most difficult to talk to, as it is hard to get any feedback: blue-vectored people just listen and prefer not to talk. With that said, pulling one over on them will probably not work — nature has made them wise, so they have already guessed your little game before you even make your first move.

People like this are very tactful: they do not argue, insist on getting their way (although they always do have an opinion), try to prove other people wrong, or worry about sorting out relationships. Blue-vectored people quit by quietly setting their resignation on their boss's desk and walking out without feeling any need for an explanation. Blue-vectored clients who are dissatisfied with a product or service do not make a fuss; they just walk out the door and find another option.

There are no key words to use when talking with the blue vector per se. However, there are "key" voices that can even be psychotherapeutic: the low, soft, velvety ones characteristic of the black and red vectors. The opposite is also true, with high, loud, squealing voices (imbalanced orange + yellow) or, alternatively, boring voices (brown + violet) acting like psychotraumatic nails on a chalkboard. Blue-vectored people do their best to stay away from people with that kind of voice. If you would like to develop a good relationship, speak softly and slowly, never forcing them into a conversation.

Blue-vectored people can sense other people's character and state of mind by listening to their voice, so be sincere when you talk to them. When we lie, some muscles responsible for voice timbre tighten — blue-vectored people and their strong sense of hearing can catch that nearly imperceptible difference. That is why it does not make sense to lie to them, especially since you will never know that you were found out. Green-vectored people can sometimes tell if a person is lying by looking into their eyes or seeing something else about them, though they say something immediately: "I think you're lying to me..." Blue-vectored people say nothing about their conjectures, choosing instead to draw their own conclusions in silence.

They make good, reliable friends who can keep secrets and are not arrogant. Their only weakness is their thoughtlessness: sometimes blue-vectored people draw so far inside themselves that they do not notice when people are offended or even start to cry. That inattention saves them from emotional overload, since hearing *absolutely* everything around them would make them go crazy.

Blue-vectored people have a very good, intelligent sense of humor: they understand any joke you throw at them, though you would never hear them resort to dirty jokes or language.

Since they talk so little, try periodically asking them what they think, or risk never finding out. Also remember that calling them at 11 pm is perfectly fine, though doing so at 10 am would be very impolite.

A SHRILL WORLD ON THE INSIDE

Blue-vectored children are very good at memorizing poems, though a good rhythm is much more important to them than the meaning:

'Twas brillig, and the slithy toves

Did gyre and gimble in the wabe;

All nimsy were the borogroves,

And the mome raths outgrabe.

Louis Carroll, Alice in Wonderland

Children like this do have problems with spelling, however, because they spell words the way they hear them. That issue follows them all the way through adulthood, meaning that they have to learn "two" languages at once. The same is true of foreign languages: blue-vectored people's brains remember both the way words are written and how they are spelled instead of memorizing a single unit.

Blue-vectored children are very quiet, do not talk much, and prefer solitude to noisy playrooms. They do not yell, scream, stamp, or wave their arms around when they are angry; the hurt stays inside, as they calmly head to their corner and cry dry tears.

Once they get older, they find an outlet in music. Their entire home becomes their auditorium, and their car is outfitted with eight speakers on the left side to match the eight on the right... Blue-vectored teenagers sometimes spend significant amounts of time listening to their headphones, although that is more a defense mechanism against an encroaching world of noise than a desire to ignore those around them.

Blue-vectored people who delve deep into themselves sometimes think they are the center of a World of Sounds, with noises hurtling at them from all sides. That leads to an interesting tendency: "I am the Center of the World of Sounds" → "I am the Center of the World" → "I am the Center" → "I..." (egocentrism[31]).

Egocentrism is an important quality of the blue vector, though it should not be confused with narcissism[32]. Narcissists (in the narrowest sense of the word) adore themselves and could not care less about others. People who are egocentric, on the other hand, may even hate themselves, though they will still feel like they are the center of a noisy, screaming, crying universe — not the most pleasant place to be.

Of course, the most unpleasant noises out there happen in major industrial cities, where life for blue-vectored people can be absolutely unbearable. Just imagine: they cannot go to sleep until 1:30 am and then wake up at 5 am, all because subway trains go roaring by every two minutes! Even beyond that, they hear the water dripping from the faucet in the building across from theirs and the cat clawing at the upstairs neighbor's carpet...even though it is three floors up. Pipes rumble, wires hum, and little insects are constantly copulating in the carpet. The heart beats still stronger,

---

[31] Egocentrism is when someone thinks they are the central object in life or their relationships.

[32] Narcissism is a behavior defined entirely by a fixation on one's own benefit and profit, putting one's self ahead of others. The opposite of narcissism is generally considered to be altruism, though that is not always the case.

and how loud the blood is rushing through the veins...

Green-vectored people who do not want to see something can close their eyes. Violet-vectored people have it a bit harder: if they do not want to clamp their fingers over their nose, they have to sneeze a few times to get rid of a smell. Blue-vectored people have no way out: even sticking earplugs in their ears is not enough to shut out the world around them. Sometimes they cannot handle the onslaught of sounds anymore and resort to extreme measures like poking holes in their own eardrums just to get a break. Of course, blue-vectored people are more comfortable living in nature, where all the noises are more harmonic and they have the ability to live in silence at least once in a while.

Now try imagining what a combination of the blue and red vectors in one person would look like. The red vector is hot, active, energetic, and sexual; the blue vector is cold, passive, inactive, and not sexual at all. The combination is like oil and water: no matter how much you stir, they still do not mix. Oddly enough, the whole problem comes down to the fact that blue-vectored people have very little uric acid, while red-vectored people have a ton of it. Sadly, there is no middle ground, and people with two different powers inside them are torn into pieces. Several times a day periods of brightness and activity are replaced by times when the person wants to retreat back into a corner and avoid seeing or hearing anything. That continuous variation leads to a terrible emotional depression that one day becomes even worse than death itself. The person commits suicide in a way that is both quiet thanks to the blue vector and inventive thanks to the red vector — the combination of blue and red is the one most prone to suicide. Alternatively, they turn to the narcotics that are widespread in the red- and blue-vector world of musicians to shut out the harrowing sensation.

If people with those vectors understand and accept both of them, they become much more stable. They will never be a phlegmatic (like their black- or brown-vectored friends), though they will not have that soul-devouring depression deep down inside.

Children with both the blue and red vectors also have a special kind of character and are sometimes called "indigo children." Their features match the description of the red vector (hyperactivity, an attention deficit, and weak concentration) as well as that of the blue vector (depth, intuition, "connection with the cosmos," and an ability to deeply understand people, things, and events).

CRAZY IS AS CRAZY DOES

I would like to finish this chapter with a story about a blue-vectored person. He is not the picture of mental health — really the opposite — though his way of life is a great descriptor of the blue vector.

I once knew a young man who had a strong blue vector I would even call off the charts. His behavior might seem deeply pathological to many, though he was quite happy with his life.

He went several perfectly healthy years without ever leaving his house. A talented programmer, he worked from home on his computer. He was paid online, and the money that came in went out the same way when he ordered groceries and everything else he needed. He chatted with his friends over the computer and made love the same way. At noon he got up and sat down at his computer, and with only a few short food and bathroom breaks he would only stop to go to sleep just before sunrise. The next day was always more of the same.

Once the electricity went out in his apartment for a few hours. When his computer stopped working he laid down on the couch and felt like he was dying. In fact, that was exactly what he said: "I'll bet people feel like this right after they die — as if all contact with the world was torn away in an instant..."

FILMS TO WATCH (WITH BLUE-VECTORED CHARACTERS)

- Dancer in the Dark, directed by Lars von Trier, Denmark and elsewhere, 2000 (Selma Jezkov, played by Björk)

- The Pianist, directed by Roman Polanski, France and elsewhere, 2002 (Wladyslaw Szpilman, played by Adrien Brody)

- Melancholia, directed by Lars von Trier, Denmark and elsewhere, 2011 (Justine, played by Kirsten Dunst)

- The Sixth Sense, directed by M. Night Shyamalan, USA, 1999 (Cole Sear, played by Haley Joel Osment)

Visit my site www.psy8.net to enjoy the Vector Test, the Vector Gallery (pictures, movies and citations of all eight vectors), the article about the compatibility of vectors, answers to readers' questions, and more.

CHAPTER 9. THE VIOLET VECTOR — NOSE

STRATEGIC GUARD

This vector, just like the red one, is easier to look at it in the context of an ancient troop of our ancestors, due primarily to the fact that the ability to perceive smells is the oldest of all the senses known to living things. The first little creatures on the planet when life first appeared were able to neither see nor hear. All the information they had was acquired through their sense of smell: they used olfaction to look for food and each other, defend themselves from danger, and find a comfortable place to live. Fast-forward millions of years, and we have people still today who live the same way.

While green-vectored (day watchmen) and blue-vectored (night watchmen) people detect danger from a good 3-5 kilometers away, that is not always good enough. That is why the troop needs someone called a "strategic guard" who is able to sniff out danger long before it gets close enough to be a threat.

According to science, mosquitos can sense the presence of humans from eleven kilometers away by smelling a single molecule. When we walk into a forest and get accosted by a cloud of them a few hours later, we did not just happen across where they were already buzzing around; it took them that long to fly those eleven kilometers.

Returning to the topic at hand, people like that are dominated by their sense of smell and in our system are grouped into the violet vector.

You can take the Vector Test on my site www.psy8.net

Viktor Tolkachev called this the "olfactory" vector and described it as follows:

People like this sit on a high hill and smell the air wafting up to them. If they were with everyone else by the fire where the meat is roasting (and a friend was sitting next to them after going a couple weeks without bathing), they would not be able to do their job. Instead, they are most often loners who sit a ways away from the group. Because having people nearby means they cannot fulfil their main function, purple-vectored people hate the entire "stinking" troop. And who is the main "stinker"? The red-vectored leader, of course, who reeks of the pheromones[33] that come with his power. As a result, violet-vectored people cannot stand alphas.

This vector's attitude is beautifully described in Patrick Süskind's *Perfume: The Story of a Murderer*[34]:

In the period of which we speak, there reigned in the cities a stench barely conceivable to us modern men and women. The streets stank of manure, the courtyards of urine, the stairwells stank of

---

[33] Pheromones are chemicals that give off a smell and are produced by people and animals. The oldest chemical compound in nature, they act on the subconscious of the surrounding people (or animals) to incite desire or passion.

[34] In 2006 an eponymous movie was filmed based on *Perfume: The Story of a Murderer*. In my opinion, it is the only instance in all of cinematography where audio and video can act on the audience's sense of smell.

moldering wood and rat droppings, the kitchens of spoiled cabbage and mutton fat; the unaired parlors stank of stale dust, the bedrooms of greasy sheets, damp featherbeds, and the pungently sweet aroma of chamber pots. The stench of sulfur rose from the chimneys, the stench of caustic lyes from the tanneries, and from the slaughterhouses came the stench of congealed blood. People stank of sweat and unwashed clothes; from their mouths came the stench of rotting teeth, from their bellies that of onions, and from their bodies, if they were no longer very young, came the stench of rancid cheese and sour milk and tumorous disease. The rivers stank, the marketplaces stank, the churches stank, it stank beneath the bridges and in the palaces. The peasant stank as did the priest, the apprentice as did his master's wife, the whole of the aristocracy stank, even the king himself stank, stank like a rank lion, and the queen like an old goat, summer and winter.

Just imagine a life like that, with everyone and everything reeking all around! The only smell that is pleasant to someone in the middle of an existence like that would be their own. Sometimes they may accept their mother's, and every now and again their father's, but everyone else stinks and is treated accordingly. They love only themselves, as the only person who smells good.

If the violet vector is not accepted, people like this are complete narcissists and misanthropes (people who hate other people) walking around with disdain written all over their faces.

COLOR, TASTE, AND SMELL

Try to count how many different colors you can name. Only list the ones that have their own, non-derivative ("burnt sienna" is the color of burnt sienna), and non-hybrid (grayish-brownish raspberry) names: red, yellow, green, blue, black, brown, gray... You can probably think of 15-20 (green-vectored people, of course, will have a few more than everyone else).

Next go ahead and think of how many words you have for taste. Only use tastes that have their own name, rather than tasting like a particular ingredient ("vanilla" is the taste of vanilla): sour, sweet, bitter... Spicy and tart are more tactile senses in the mouth, as opposed to tastes. Regardless, the point is that we have fewer words for tastes than we do for colors.

But how many words do you think we have for smells? Here we can only use dedicated words themselves, avoiding the smell of something in particular like the sea. Neither can we borrow from tastes to say something like "a sweet smell." It turns out that looking for words that purely describe smells leaves us empty-handed. "Fragrant" and "stinking" assess smells instead of naming them: a man's armpit has a pleasant aroma if you ask his loving wife, while other women think it smells terrible.

Not a single one of our planet's languages have words for smells. Even the Native Americans, who are said to have had a script for smells that assigned different designations to different smells, did not have words for those smells themselves.

It turns out that violet-vectored people think differently than the rest of us, as they do not go off of concepts. Each of us has a special world of smells that is nearly impossible to describe, something that explains many of the violet vector's qualities.

FOLLOWING THEIR GUT

All violet-vectored people dream of finding their favorite scent, one they long ago smelled or perhaps simply imagined. And if they find it, they will do anything to stay close to it.

We can go back to Patrick Süskind:

> *Normally human odor was nothing special, or it was ghastly. Children smelled insipid, men urinous, all sour sweat and cheese, women smelled of rancid fat and rotting fish. Totally uninteresting, repulsive — that was how humans smelled... And so it happened that for the first time in his life, Grenouille did not trust his nose and had to call on his eyes for assistance if he was to believe what he smelled [a girl was walking in front of him]. ... And now he smelled that this was a human being, smelled the sweat of her armpits, the oil in her hair, the fishy odor of her genitals, and smelled it all with the greatest pleasure.*

> *... and the harmony of all these components yielded a perfume so rich, so balanced, so magical, that every perfume that Grenouille had smelled until now, every edifice of odors that he had so playfully created within himself, seemed at once to be utterly meaningless. A hundred thousand odors seemed worthless in the presence of this scent. ... It was pure beauty.*

> *... He wanted to press, to emboss this apotheosis of scent on his black, muddled soul, meticulously to explore it and from this point on, to think, to live, to smell only according to the innermost structures of its magic formula.*

Süskind's main character also had a black vector (in deep

neurosis, no less) equally as strong as his violet vector, which is why it did not matter to him whether the girl was dead or alive. Violet-vectored people do not commit crimes themselves, however, so he will use someone else to do the deed.

Let us imagine that we are an ancient troop of anthropoid apes. Every day we eat bananas, and at some point we just get tired of them. That is when our red-vectored alpha, who always takes the branch less swung, tells us that we are moving out in search of a pineapple grove. We are happy and satisfied, eating novel and delicious pineapples.

But then a violet-vectored ape comes over to the red-vectored alpha and whispers to him, "I'm not 100% sure if it's a leopard or a lion, but something is definitely ten kilometers away. Though maybe it's nothing..." The alpha is used to trusting the violet-vectored ape's nose, and so he gives the command: "So much for the pineapples, we're heading back to the banana grove." Dejected, we slink out of the trees and follow him back to eat the same old bananas.

Here is the question: who is the real leader of the troop? The power broker! Put it this way: you have seen quite a few spider webs, but far fewer spiders. Violet-vectored people are like spiders who spin their webs, ensnare the entire troop, and sit in a corner pulling strings until everyone is marching to the beat of their drum. Of course, two spiders cannot share a single web, and one usually eats the other — most often females make short work of the males. Even when their violet vectors are equal, women generally beat out men in the backroom struggle for control of the system.

Violet-vectored instigators are not even capable of finding a worm to catch a fish with; instead, they feed off the troop.

LIVING IN A SMELLY WORLD

Imagine a violet-vectored child riding a hot bus: his nose would be right at waist level with the red- and black-vectored men around him. That is why children like that barely breathe when taking public transportation, preferring oxygen starvation. If they are on their way to class, they will have a hard time collecting their thoughts until they have had a chance to "catch their breath" a few hours later.

Riding the subway in the summer is awful for violet-vectored people. They zigzag through the entrance hall, making sure there are a few yards between them and the people who smell the worst. When the train arrives they take a deep breath, hold it, and get on board with eyes bulging from the effort. They usually do not sit down (for the same reason: they would be at waist level), standing instead by the doors and trying to grasp at the little fresh air that sneaks in (if you see someone in the subway with bulging eyes, do not jump to the conclusion that they are green-vectored; they may just be trying to hold their breath). As soon as the doors open at the next station, they stick their head out and start gulping down air before taking a deep breath and doing the same thing all over again. Look down the length of your train during the heat of summer and you will be sure to see a row of noses sticking out of the open doors hungry for fresh air. Crowds of hot people are torture for the violet-vectored ones among them.

Viktor Tolkachev once told a similar "summer" story. It was a Friday night and he was on the subway in a half-full car. At one stop a green- and violet-vectored girl got on and stood near the door, followed at the next stop by two construction workers on their way home to get a shower. They noticed the cute girl and came to stand next to her. Her eyes were already quite large, and once the two guys in their dirty overalls came over they began getting bigger and bigger. She was doing her best not to breathe, but the next station did not come fast enough... Finally she took a deep breath and suddenly...turned pale and slowly sank to the floor. The young men, not taken aback, caught her, set her on the bench, and start buzzing around, their hands clumsily patting her cheeks. The girl got even whiter... "Had I not been on the train," said Tolkachev, "those two guys would have smothered her..."

HABITS

Violet-vectored people have no need for luxury in their lives —all they need is normal comfort (secretly managing other people is luxury enough for them).

Their favorite color, of course, is violet, and their favorite shape is the zigzag. However, they are too concerned about keeping their vector hidden to wear violet-colored clothes.

Needless to say, sneezing is a violet-vector pleasure that could almost be classified as a "nasal orgasm." Violet-vectored people sometimes sneeze multiple times in a row, blow their nose, and then sneeze again. Incidentally, snuff tobacco was developed with this vector in mind. Violet-vectored people also love touching their nose, while children (and some adults) get a huge kick out of picking it.

A boy and his father come home from the zoo, and the boy, in tears, tells his mom, "I felt so bad for the horse...he didn't have fingers to pick his nose with..." Who but a violet-vectored child would understand the horse's tragedy?

Violet-vectored people find the world of aromas fascinating: not only perfumeries, but also incense, scented oils, and everything else. Be careful, however, about giving them aromatic presents: only do so if you are absolutely sure they like that particular scent. Otherwise your gift will be thrown in the trash the minute the door closes behind you.

They take selecting a new fragrance very seriously, sometimes spending hours at the store testing bottle after bottle. Other violet-vectored people, on the other hand, cannot imagine anything better than their own scent, and so they never go to perfume stores (though this does not mean that they smell strongly). Incidentally, those latter ones have a habit of sticking their nose in their own armpits.

Sometimes the love they have for their own scent turns pathological. One client told me how she lives alone and changes her sheets twice a year. "In this giant world there are only 15 square feet that always smell like me. That is where I belong." I should say that she was absolutely clean (given her brown vector), and in all other areas was well-adapted.

Can you imagine how difficult it is for violet-vectored people to visit other people? And inviting others to visit them is probably even harder. When you visit someone else, you can always go home and wash the smell off; it takes weeks to air out your own place after other people come to visit...

That is why violet-vectored people usually do not invite people over to visit, and tend not to visit others. If they decide to do so, they do not immediately ring the doorbell when they arrive.

Instead they sniff to see if anyone they would rather avoid is there, in which case they turn around and go home. Obviously, that all happens subconsciously for the most part, though the fact of their behavior remains the same.

I remember a birthday party I was at once. Everyone was there except for one last person, and we soon saw him through the window — he was on his way to the house holding a cake and a bouquet of flowers. But the doorbell did not ring in the next five minutes, or in the ten after that. Finally, worried that something had happened, we called him: "I didn't feel good, so I went home." We saw right through that: a few fallen petals on the mat made it clear that he had been at the door. That was a bit odd though, since real violet-vectored people cover their tracks...

PROFESSIONS AND WORK

Violet-vectored people are curious, if very careful. At work their curiosity takes on an intellectual flavor, while their interests and abilities cast a wide net: perfumers and chemists; meteorologists and psychologists; special agents, customs inspectors, and ecologists; parodists and satirists; and diplomats and informants ("rats" — Viktor Tolkachev said that ratting out other people is a way of taking revenge on the stinking members of the troop).

The sommelier[35] profession is especially interesting. They are taught at special schools how to break wine aromas down into

---

[35] A sommelier is the person at a restaurant responsible for purchasing, storing, and serving wine to the patrons. They present the wine menu, handle degustation, and offer drink recommendations.

their individual components and interpret the result. Professionals can determine the quality, sort, and sometimes even the region and age of wine just from smelling it.

Doctors with violet vectors make for excellent diagnosticians, as they are intuitive and can tell diseases apart by smell.

There is even an old joke about doctors like this. One is doing the rounds, talking to all his patients before he finishes his shift: "John, see you later! Peter, talk to you soon! James, goodbye..." There is an even darker version of this joke: "All right, you'll be meeting with Dr. Jones on Monday, James." "Who is that?!" "Our coroner..."

Violet-vectored people are the top-notch advisors and assistants who stand behind red-vectored leaders — though they despise them for the way they reek of power, they still need them. After all, violet-vectored people can only implement their ideas through a red-vectored leader. They do not need symbols of power, knowing quite well that they hold the real thing in their hands; the crown and scepter are for red-vectored leaders to show their power and draw attention to themselves. With that said, red-vectored people are always in the public eye, which limits them. Violet-vectored people work from the shadows, meaning they have no limits.

So why do red-vectored people trust their violet-vectored assistants? They probably can guess that their headlong recklessness could force them to eventually make a mistake, something they absolutely cannot afford (remember: "Akela missed!"). These two people complement each other perfectly, even if they cannot stand each other — the combination simply cannot be beaten.

Of course, leaders who have both vectors at once are lucky: they are capable of managing people openly (directly) and secretly. The combination does have its drawbacks, however: the red vector is prone to risk-taking and going full speed ahead, while the violet vector is always holding it back — "Are you sure you've thought this through? Have you foreseen every alternative? What if something happens?"

The combination of violet and orange (intuition plus logic) is also another excellent one for many different areas, from business to scientific research, so long as both are accepted.

CONVERSATION

Violet-vectored people familiarize themselves with new people using their nose. If they do not like their new friend's smell, they will have nothing to do with her personally or professionally (no matter how valuable she could be).

Never lie to violet-vectored people. While green-vectored people can see you lying by looking you in the eye, and their blue-vectored friends can hear it in your voice, violet-vectored people can smell your lie before you even open your mouth. No sooner does it come into your head to say it than the corresponding pheromones you release instantly give you away.

Be sure to shower thoroughly before meeting violet-vectored people. On the other hand, avoid overdoing it! If you wash off your natural scent completely, you will come across as incomprehensible and dangerous.

Violet-vectored children are master manipulators. Even at a young age they can push the buttons of their parents, caretakers, and teachers. At kindergarten they start by tattling (an immature form of manipulation), after which they begin expertly creating intrigue. If a child like this does not like how his teacher smells, he will find a way to get her replaced — she will eventually leave the class, though no one will know who was really responsible. But what if the child does not like how his father smells (a scary thought!)? It will not be long before the unlucky father is pushed out of the family, though, again, nobody will know who the real driver was. Violet-vectored people always manage to walk away with no one the wiser.

APPEARANCE AND OTHER FEATURES

Violet-vectored people are usually thin, and they do their best to dress plainly (they are reminiscent of their blue-vectored friends in this area). Their faces can be haughty and somewhat contemptuous: the corners of their mouths are a bit turned down, while their eyes are lightly squinted.

Their most important feature, of course, is their nose, which can be large or unusually shaped. With that said, do not forget that the most violet-vectored of them may have a nose that would never attract attention. Looking at their sweet face, it would not even cross your mind that you are standing in front of a master manipulator who knows everything you are about to do before you even do it.

Sometimes they hang their sweater over their nose to keep

strange smells out and better smell themselves.

When possible, violet-vectored people leave doors cracked behind them, something that can be seen as a subconscious attempt to give themselves an escape route. They spend quite of bit of energy creating back doors at work, in their private lives, and so on.

Violet-vector handwriting is most often illegible — sometimes they themselves cannot figure out what they wrote. In that case they hold the piece of paper up to their nose, wave it around slowly, and wait until they remember what they wrote.

Illegible handwriting characterizes the violet vector for a reason: their guiding principle in life is to never leave traces behind them. They prefer to avoid having their picture taken, showing up in videos, giving autographs, and signing documents. Recently I heard a fantastic phrase from a young man with a remarkable nose sitting at the next table in a restaurant: "I'll sleep easy when there isn't a single document left that points back to me." I so wanted to whisper to his neighbor: "Be careful!"

Violet-vector humor is sharp and sometimes malicious: irony, satire, and sarcasm. People like this love groups where everyone laughs at each other's expense — that happens to also be the only place you can crack a joke about a violet-vectored person without worrying about the consequences. Although, who knows...

I remember getting together with a group of friends like this when I was young (there were three girls and two guys), spending a few hours absolutely shredding each other. We were not pulling any punches, especially since we had all known each other for quite a while and knew each other's weaknesses and sore spots. If anyone witnessed the event, they probably thought we were ferocious enemies ready to tear each other to pieces. As it turned out, we parted ways cheerful and rested.

LOVE AND SEX

The violet vector's sexual potential is far from high, though it depends to a large degree on the partner's scent. If that scent is neutral, the potential is very low; if it is unpleasant, the potential is zero (or even negative). However, violet-vectored people who find that scent desire their partners all day, every day.

Some violet-vectored women claim they would rather not have sex at all, since men are all "stinking jerks." It is only rarely that you can find one who smells good. On the other hand, anyone from a knock-dead looker to some kind of Quasimodo can have that smell, and so all the girlfriends often crowd around a violet-vectored woman after a dubious find: "What do you see in him?? He isn't smart, he isn't handsome, he isn't rich, he isn't anything!" And she has no way of explaining (and often herself does not understand) that he is the only one who could smell like him. In a situation like that a violet-vectored woman might mention that he is the only man in whose armpit she can curl up and go to sleep.

However, even one's favorite scent comes with problems. When violet-vectored people fall in love with their partner's smell, there is no going back. Beat them, kick them, make fun of them — they will go nowhere. No matter what happens, they will stay nearby with one answer to any question that is asked: "Do what you want; just let me stay with you."

Quite a few books and movies have been based on that phrase. One could point to the tragic story of Victor Hugo's daughter in François Truffaut's The Story of Adele H. (1975). Adele Hugo fell in love with an officer unrequitedly. Not taking no for an answer, however, she followed him for 12 years across cities, countries, and even continents (France, Canada, and India) with a single phrase: "Do what you want; just let me see you." Unable to handle her attachment any longer, she spent the next 43 years of her life in a psychiatric hospital before dying there at age 85. This syndrome was later named after her[36].

A similar tragedy plays out in Roman Polanski's Bitter Moon (1992): the heroine cannot forget her passion even when her partner begins humiliating and mocking her.

It's true what I said. I can't live without you. Please, don't throw me out — give me one last chance. I'm ready to live with you on any terms, any at all! I can bear anything as long as I'm with you sometimes. You can shout at me. You can hit me. You can have other women. I don't care what you do, but please don't send me away! Even if you don't love me anymore, keep me with you out of pity... There's nothing I wouldn't do to stay with you. Please, I beg you, please...

This type of situation can also lead to homosexual love: once that long-awaited scent is found, violet-vectored people will stay with that person no matter if they are a man or a woman.

Marriages with violet-vectored people can only be happy if there is that special scent, something that happens only very rarely

---

[36] Adele Syndrome is an all-absorbing, long-lasting, amorous, harmful, and unrequited obsession and passion.

— once or twice in your lifetime if you are lucky. That is why they prefer guest marriages, which are when they visit, have a meal, sleep, play with the children, and then go back home to their natural smells. For the same reason violet-vectored men often marry women with children who are grown: they can avoid all those stinky diapers.

Many violet-vectored men who find happiness in marriage prefer when their women smell only like themselves, avoiding perfumes. They say Napoleon wrote to his wife Joséphine on his way home: "Dear, I'll be home in a week, so stop bathing."

READY OR NOT...WELL, THE VIOLET VECTOR IS ALWAYS READY

Since all our emotions have their own particular scent, violet-vectored people are great at understanding how those around them are feeling. At the same time, they are able to behave in such a way that nobody notices them in a group — it is almost as if they fade into the background. Sometimes after parties where there were 15 people everyone tries to remember who was there. They can only count 14, however, and asking around does not clear up who that last person was...

Sometimes violet-vectored people are at meetings where their colleagues are discussing an important issue. They sit quietly until the group finally makes a decision, at which point, almost as if by accident, throw out an unrelated phrase: "Oh look, it's raining..." Everyone looks out the window, talks about the rain for a bit, and then gets back to the topic at hand — but this time they come to a completely different conclusion. And who would ever guess what really happened? The thought would never cross their mind that a few adults could be led around by the nose like that.

What do you think black-vectored people do when there is a fire? They bring water, carry heavy equipment, and do what they are told.

What do red-vectored people do when there is a fire? Obviously, they direct the process, pouring the water on the fire, and carry out feats of valor.

What do brown-vectored people do when there is a fire? They put out the last embers (finish the process) to make sure it does not flare up again.

What do orange-vectored people do when there is a fire? They save their own valuables and everyone else's, afterward counting up the losses.

What do yellow-vectored people do when there is a fire? They scream, "Over here! Get that out of there! Everyone come here! Fire!!!!"

What do green-vectored people do when there is a fire? They give first aid, soothing and calming everyone else.

What do blue-vectored people do when there is a fire? This one is not as simple: they are the people who need to be saved, especially as children (they freeze under the bed or in the closet and do not even respond when called).

And what do violet-vectored people do when there is a fire? They are usually not around when fires break out, as they smell the first match before it even begins to burn and get out of there. They are the rats fleeing the ship before it hits the iceberg.

If violet-vectored people start quitting at your company, give some thought to the fact that it might be time for you to pack your bags as well. They sense financial and political crises ahead of time, keeping their nose to the wind and making sure nothing catches them by surprise.

Incidentally, violet-vectored people rarely collect a lot of points on the psychological vector test in that category. Their results are most often run-of-the-mill: all their vectors are at about the same middling level. Their acceptance of each vector is also the same and also middling. In short, the test is not a reliable indicator of violet-vectored people, something that is true of all analysis delving into their sly vector.

They rarely get straight to the point in conversations, and almost never answer yes or no. Instead, their favorite answer is "well, maybe..."

In contrast to the clairvoyant green vector and the clairaudience of the blue vector, the violet vector is blessed with an outstanding intuition. Green-vectored people see pictures that come out of nowhere, while blue-vectored people hear a voice coming from inside them; violet-vectored people hear and see nothing out of the ordinary. For example, they may be driving along the highway and suddenly decide to turn around and drive back the way they came, only to do so, look back, and see an accident that just happened.

HEALTH

Violet-vectored people have weak constitutions. Children living among uncomfortable smells suffer from a chronically stuffy nose (their adenoids develop for that purpose), while adults also deal with similar problems related to allergies, sinusitis, and other diseases "protecting" them from the unpleasant scents in their lives. Of course, this problem can be treated surgically, though that traumatizes their significant zone and therefore often leads to violet-vector neurosis.

Note that as soon as violet-vectored people get rid of the smells that bother them in their surroundings and find their favorite scent (someone's armpit or a cat, for instance), all their nasal problems go away on their own within a few days or weeks. The only difficulty is that pinpointing the smell at fault is much more difficult than finding an offending color or sound. Its source can also be anything or anyone, including a close relative who lives in the same house.

People with an unaccepted violet vector and an unaccepted orange vector may suffer from bronchial asthma. In that case, balancing both vectors will bring significant relief, sometimes even leading to a complete recovery.

Occasionally their strong olfactory sensitivity makes violet-vectored people overly suspicious. They receive so much information through their noses that they cannot always tell what is true and what is not, so they prefer to err on the side of caution: they check multiple times to make sure the electricity, gas, and water are all shut off.

Violet-vectored people are an insurance company's dream, as they like to insure everything they can in order to minimize unforeseen problems down the road. They even encrypt the data on their computers, making many copies that each have their own password.

They are equally suspicious when it comes to their own health: a tiny zit in an unusual place or a little lethargy puts them in a panic, fearing for their lives. This is further complicated by the distrust they have for doctors and sometimes everyone else.

CHARACTER AND BALANCE

When their vector is realized and satisfied, violet-vectored people are fairly pleasant and interesting to talk to. They are highly intellectual (almost to a blue-vector level), have a well-developed thought process, and wield an impressive intuition. Blue-vectored and violet-vectored people love psychology and philosophy, spend time thinking about eternal truths, and ponder the meaning of life and death. That is why they get along with each other so well.

Violet-vectored people at the table sniff their food before shoveling it into their mouths, especially as visitors. That behavior sometimes surprises their cordial hosts: "What are you smelling it for?! Everything is fresh!" They do not realize that violet-vectored people even at home do not taste the food they are preparing; instead, they smell it (a sniff to find out that it needs more salt, a pinch of salt, and one more sniff — perfect).

They are true coffee and tea aficionados, able to tell the difference between hundreds of types.

They can also remember everything that happens in their lives by associating it with a smell.

Violet-vectored people rarely play sports, preferring to stay away from the strong, unpleasant odors that always come with them. Their sport is chess, where everything is built on intuition (and orange-vector logic). Incidentally, it was chess players many years ago who thought up correspondence, phone, and internet games to avoid olfactory contact with their opponents.

CHARACTER IN NEUROSIS

An imbalanced violet vector is prone to seclusion, unprovoked irritability, and a chronic resentment of everything around it, something people with imbalanced violet vectors do not even realize is rooted in their olfactory environment. Robbed of an outlet for their needs and abilities, they may begin to cope primarily with a "studied lack of principles." That is best expressed by one of their favorite phrases: "oh, screw it all."

People for whom this vector is not accepted sometimes develop two dangerous qualities: vindictiveness and an inability to forgive. You might hurt a violet-vectored person in some small way and, of course, sincerely apologize. Most likely you will hear something like "oh, don't worry about it — we're friends, after all," though relaxing and forgetting out of naiveté would be a terrible mistake. The problem is that your violet-vectored friend will never forget that offense. Many months or even years later he will find exactly the right moment and repay you a hundred times over, which is why experienced people have some advice: "never underestimate a wounded foe." If you accidentally take a picture of a violet-vectored person without their permission (or, heaven forbid, take a video of them), I would strongly advise you to watch your step.

One more quality of an imbalanced violet vector is inveterate pessimism. Some of their favorite expressions are, "What's wrong today?", "This won't end well," "I told you so!", "The best is the enemy of the good," and "Leave well enough alone."

ONE MORE THING ABOUT SMELLS

For every last scent on Earth there is someone who enjoys it. Certainly, the smell of roses has more admirers than that of rubber shoes, but there is someone out there who really does love how rubber shoes smell. The same is true of absolutely everything else. There are even some imbalanced black- and violet-vectored people who are subconsciously drawn to the smell of death. And if that combination is joined by a red vector, which does everything on a global scale, well, you can imagine what would happen. Neurotic violet-vectored people hate everyone around them ("they all stink"), neurotic black-vectored people know how to make the problem go away ("get rid of the guy and the problem takes care of itself"), and neurotic red-vectored people add massive proportions to the sinister goal ("the end justifies the means"). You can guess how that ends yourself.

We should mention one more violet-vector peculiarity in this chapter, though it does not yet have a scientific or even logical explanation. Violet-vectored people sometimes subconsciously take on foreign scents: having spent some time chatting with someone, they notice that a little while later they begin to smell like that person. This is not even an illusion or an olfactory hallucination — even the people who are close to them can confirm that their bodily odor has changed. There is nothing controlling the process, and a few days or weeks later the foreign scent disappears. When I first came across a situation like this, I thought it was simply the fruit of an overly active imagination. However, in the past 20 years I have heard quite a few stories about similar "miracles," and always from people with strong violet vectors.

Some strongly violet-vectored people try to air out their living area frequently to get rid of strange smells. Others, on the other hand, try to keep everything closed in to hang onto their own olfactory aura. If you ever see two people arguing over whether to open a window, you are probably looking at a clash between two violet vectors.

I would like to close with a violet-vector joke.

A violet-vectored wife tells her black-vectored husband in the morning, "Honey, we're going to the theater tonight, so don't forget to change your socks." "Got it, I won't."

At some point during the day she calls him at work: "Honey, do you remember that we're going to the theater tonight? You'll change your socks, right?" "What are you worrying about? Of course I will."

That evening they are getting ready to leave: "Honey, change your socks, please!" "Okay, on it."

They get to the theater and find their seats, which is when the wife grimaces and turns to her husband: "Honey, I asked you to change your socks!" He sticks a hand into his pocket, pulls out the dirty socks, and says, "I changed them, but I knew you wouldn't believe me. Here you go!"

FILMS TO WATCH (WITH VIOLET-VECTORED CHARACTERS)

- The Story of Adele H., directed by François Truffaut, France, 1975 (Adèle Hugo, played by Isabelle Adjani)

- Bitter Moon, directed by Roman Polanski; France, UK, and USA; 1992 (Mimi, played by Emmanuelle Seigner)

- Scent of a Woman, directed by Dino Risi, Italy, 1974 (Il capitano Fausto Consolo, played by Vittorio Gassman)

- Perfume: The Story of a Murderer, directed by Tom Tykwer; Germany, France, Spain, and USA; 2006 (Jean-Baptiste Grenouille, played by Ben Whishaw)

- The Talented Mr. Ripley, directed by Anthony Minghella, USA, 1999 (Tom Ripley, played by Matt Damon)

- Léon: The Professional, directed by Luc Besson, France, 1994 (Stansfield, played by Gary Oldman)

- Disclosure, directed by Barry Levinson, USA, 1994 (Meredith Johnson, played by Demi Moore)

Visit my site www.psy8.net to enjoy the Vector Test, the Vector Gallery (pictures, movies and citations of all eight vectors), the article about the compatibility of vectors, answers to readers' questions, and more.

CONCLUSION

And there you have it, your first encounter with psychological vectors has come to an end, leaving you with undoubtedly many questions.

- How do you determine your dominant vectors when you see aspects of yourself in each description?

- How do you differentiate one vector from another when they share striking similarities?

- How do you engage with someone who exhibits numerous vivid vectors or, conversely, appears to have less pronounced ones?

- How do you distinguish one vector's neurosis from the intense expression of another?

These and many other questions often linger in the minds of most individuals after acquainting themselves with vector theory. To find answers and swiftly transform your knowledge into skills, you can take the following steps:

1. Visit the Vector Gallery on the website www.psy8.net. There, you will find photographs, quotes, and brief articles about vectors that will help you better immerse yourself in this system.

2. Start applying this knowledge today: observe those around you, make assumptions, and then, within minutes, confirm (or refute) your hypotheses. In no time, you'll become adept

at identifying vectors almost on the spot.

3. Engage in conversations with friends who have read this book. Through such interactions, in debates and discussions, you will gain a profound understanding of your own and others' vectors. This is precisely what my colleagues and I did during Viktor Tolkachev's training sessions back in 1994.

4. Work on accepting your own vectors because doing so enables you to accurately perceive vectors in others and subconsciously select the most effective communication style with them.

If you wish to delve deeper into psychological vectors and use this methodology for self-realization, building harmonious relationships, financial growth, or managing people, subscribe to my newsletter (www.psy8.net/subscribe) to be notified when my online vector training in English becomes available.

This training doesn't merely reiterate the knowledge presented in this book; it represents a continuation and expansion of vector theory. It includes lessons, engaging tasks, as well as regular online meetings where I'll address your questions and assist you in resolving the most challenging situations.

I wish you numerous new discoveries in your self-exploration and in understanding others!

Michael Borodiansky

APPENDIX 1. ALPHABETICAL LIST OF CHARACTER TRAITS AND EXTERNAL FEATURES

Accusations — orange, (red)

Activity — red, orange, yellow

Agalmatophilia — green

Aggression — red, black, yellow

Alacrity — red, yellow

Alarmism — yellow

Alcohol (addiction) — red

Alcohol (high tolerance) — black

Alcohol (low tolerance) — green, blue

Altruism — red

Ambition — red

Amorousness — red, green

Arrogance — violet

Artistry — yellow, green

Attention (to detail) — brown, blue

Attention (to people) — brown, green

Audial — blue

Authoritativeness — red

Avarice — orange

Bashfulness — brown, green

Belief in God — green, black

Belief in miracles — green

Belief in one's self — red

Belief in people — green

Biting — yellow

Boasting — red, yellow

Boldness — red, (black)

Canines — yellow

Cannibalism — yellow

Care — brown, green

Careerism — red

Carefree — yellow

Carelessness — red, yellow

Cheerfulness — yellow, red, orange

Clairvoyance — green

Cleanliness — brown

Clumsiness — black

Collectivism — black

Compliments (giving) — yellow, green

Compliments (love hearing) — red, green, yellow

Concentration — brown, black, orange

Conflict (proneness to) — black, red (yellow)

Conscientiousness — brown

Conservatism — brown, black

Contempt — violet

Controllability — black, green

Coquetry — green

Courage — black (red)

Creativity — red, yellow

Cruelty — black (brown)

Culture — green, blue

Cunning — violet

Curiosity — green, violet, yellow

Cursing — yellow, black, red

Cynicism — red, violet

Decency — brown, blue, green

Decorations — green

Demonstrative — green

Dependence (on people) — black, green

Dependence (on alcohol, drugs or gambling games) — red

Depression — red, blue (red + blue!)

Depth (of feeling) — blue

Destructiveness — black

Diligence — brown

Diplomacy — green, blue, violet

Discipline — orange

Disinterestedness — green (red)

Disorder — red, yellow

Disorganization — red, yellow

Dissatisfaction — violet, (orange)

Distrustfulness — violet

Doubts — violet

Earrings — green + blue

Eccentricity — green + red

Economy — orange

Egocentrism — blue

Egoism — red, violet

Emotionality — yellow, green

Empathy — green

Endurance — black, orange

Energy — red, yellow

Enthusiasm — red, yellow

Erudition — green, blue, violet

Exhibitionism — green

Falsity — violet, (yellow)

Fearfulness — green

Femininity — green

Fickleness — red

Fidelity (to one's partner) — brown, black, blue

First place — red

Flabbiness — blue, violet

Flattery — violet

Flexibility (of thought) — red, yellow, green

Flightiness — red, yellow, green

Foresight — violet

Frailty — green, blue, violet

Freedom — red

Friendliness — yellow, green

Frivolity — red, yellow

Fussiness — red, yellow

Generosity — red, green

Genius — red + any vector

Gluttony — yellow

Goodwill — green

Gourmet — yellow

Graphomania — brown

Guilt — orange + green

Habit of getting stuck — brown

Harshness — red, black

Haste — red

Hatred — violet

Headphones — blue

Helplessness — green, blue

Homosexuality (f) — black, orange (red)

Homosexuality (m) — green + brown

Honesty — brown

Hot body — red

Hot temper — red, yellow

Hot-blooded — red

Humility — black, orange + green

Humor — red, yellow, violet

Hypersexuality — red

Hypnotizability — black, green

Hysteria — green

Imagination — yellow, green

Immorality — red, violet

Impatience — red, yellow

Impetuosity — red, yellow

Impulsiveness — red, yellow, green

Inattentiveness — red, yellow, blue

Indecision — brown, black, green

Independence — red

Infantilism — green, black

Infidelity — red

Ingenuity — red, yellow

Initiative — red

Innovation — red

Inquisitiveness — green, violet

Intrigue — violet

Inventiveness — red

Irony — violet

Irresponsibility — yellow (green, black)

Irritability — violet, (orange, red)

Jealousy — red, orange, violet

Justice — brown

Kindness — green (yellow)

Kissing — yellow

Law-abiding — brown, black, orange, green

Laziness — yellow, (red, green, blue)

Leadership — red, (yellow)

Left-handedness — blue

Logic — orange

Loyalty — brown, black

Luck — red

Lying — violet, (yellow)

Manipulation — violet, orange

Masochism — orange

Melancholy — blue, violet

Memory (good) — brown, green, blue, violet

Meteosensitivity — blue

Meticulousness — brown

Misanthropy — violet

Modesty — brown, black, blue

Monotony — black

Moralism — orange

Morality — orange

Naiveté — green, black

Narcissism — green

Negligence — red, yellow

Nodding (of head) — blue

Obedience — black, orange

Obligation — brown, orange

Obsessive — brown

Optimism — yellow (red, green)

Orderliness — brown

Pain tolerance — orange, black

Parasitism — violet

Patience — brown, blue

Patriotism — black

Peacefulness — green, blue, (yellow)

Pedantry — brown

Pessimism — violet

Philanthropy — green, (red)

Phlegmatic — brown, black

Piercings — green + orange

Planning — brown, orange

Pliability — green

Plumpness (bodily) — yellow

Ponytail (hairstyle) — orange

Practicality — brown, red, orange

Presentiment — green, blue, violet

Pride — red

Principles (strong) — black (orange, brown)

Quiet voice — blue

Rationality — orange

Rebelliousness — red

Receptiveness — green, blue

Recklessness — red

Red hair — orange

Refinement — green + blue

Reliability — brown, black

Religion — green, black (orange)

Respect (to other people) — green, brown

Responsibility — brown, orange, (red)

Restraint — orange, blue, violet

Reverie — green, (red, yellow)

Rigidity — black (orange, brown)

Risk — red

Sacrifice — green + orange

Sadism — brown

Sanguine — red, orange

Sarcasm — violet

Scrupulousness — brown

Self-control — black, orange

Selflessness — orange, black, red

Self-sacrifice — orange, black, red

Sense of duty — orange (black)

Sensitivity — green, blue, violet

Sensuality — green + red, blue + red

Sentimentality — green

Sexuality — red

Shyness — green, blue, brown

Sickliness — green, blue, violet

Simplicity — black

Sincerity — green

Slander — violet

Slouch — blue

Slovenliness — red, yellow

Sluggishness — brown, blue

Smoking — yellow

Sociability — yellow, green (red)

Solitude — blue, violet

Sophistication — green + blue, green + violet

Speed — red

Spirituality — blue

Sports — black, orange

Squeamishness — brown, violet

Stability — black, brown

Stinginess — orange

Strength (physical) — black

Stubbornness — brown, black

Stylishness (in clothing) — green

Submission — black, orange + green

Successfulness — red

Suggestibility — black, green

Suspiciousness — violet

Sympathy — green

Tactfulness — green, blue

Talkativeness — yellow

Tattoos — green + orange

Teamwork — black

Tearfulness — green

Tediousness — brown

Tenderness — green, blue

Theatricality — green

Thinness — green, blue, violet

Thoroughness — brown

Thrift — brown, orange

Tickling — orange

Tidiness — brown

Tolerance — blue

Tongue clucking — yellow

Touchiness — green, violet (brown)

Tranquility — brown, black

Treachery — violet

Trustfulness — black, green

Uncertainty — brown (green)

Unpredictability — red, violet

Unscrupulousness — violet

Unselfishness — red (black, green)

Vanity — red

Vengefulness — violet

Verbal intellect — yellow

Vindictiveness — violet

Vivacity — red, yellow, green

Voyeurism — green

Vulnerability — green, violet, brown

Weakness — green, blue, violet

Whistling — yellow

Willpower — black, orange

Wisdom — blue

Wit (sharp) — violet, red, yellow

APPENDIX 2. ALPHABETICAL LIST OF HABITS AND HOBBIES

Alcohol — red, (yellow)

Antiques (collecting) — brown, orange, green

Astrology — blue + orange, violet + orange

Astronomy — blue + green

Ballet — orange + blue + green

Bathing (in a tub) — red

Biking — brown (orange)

Billiards — orange + red

Birds (pets) — green, blue

Bowling — black + orange

Boxing — black

Casinos — red

Cats — orange

Chess — violet

Cleaning — brown

Coffee — yellow, violet

Collecting — brown

Concerts (dancing) — black, orange + blue

Concerts (listening) — blue

Concerts (watching) — green

Conversation — yellow, green

Cooking — yellow

Crossword puzzles — brown, orange

Dancing — (black), orange + blue

Design — green

Dieting — brown, orange

Diving — red + green

Dogs (pets) — brown, black

Dominoes — brown, orange

Drugs (hard) — red

Drugs (soft) — green, blue, violet

Embroidery — brown, green

Enemas — brown

Equestrian sports — brown, black

Fashion — green

Fasting — orange

Fencing — orange

Fishing (sedentary) — brown

Fishing (sport) — red

Fish-keeping (aquarium) — green

Fitness — black, orange

Flowers — green

Fragrances — violet

Gardening — black + green

Graffiti — green + red

Horse racing — red, black

Horses — brown, black

Housekeeping — brown

Ice swimming — orange

Inventing — red

Karaoke — yellow

Kayaking — black, red

Keeping a diary — brown

Kleptomania — orange

Knitting — brown

Languages (study) — yellow, blue

Laying on the couch — red, yellow (green, blue)

Mafia (game) — violet

Massages — black, orange

Meditation — black + blue

Money-lending — orange

Monopoly (game) — orange (red)

Mountaineering — red

Museums — green, (blue)

Music — blue

Operas — blue + green

Paintball — red, orange, black

Painting — green

Partying — black, red, yellow, green

Philanthropy — green, (red)

Philately — brown + green

Philosophy — blue, violet

Photography — green

Promiscuity — red

Psychology — blue, violet, (green)

Racing — red

Rallying — red

Raw foodism — orange

Reading — brown

Roulette — red

Running — black, orange

Russian roulette — red

Sales — orange

Sauna — orange

Sewing — brown, orange

Shooting — orange

Shopping — orange, green

Singing — yellow

Skydiving — red

Smoking — yellow (violet)

Soccer — black + orange

Solitude — blue, violet

Speleology — red + brown (black)

Sports — black, orange

Sports (watching) — black

Swimming — red + black, red + orange

Tattoos — orange + green

Tea — yellow, violet

Theater — green, blue

Tourism (hiking) — black + red

Traveling — red, green, (yellow)

TV shows — green

Vegetarianism — orange

Vodka — red, black

Wine — yellow, violet

Winter swimming — orange

Workaholism — black

Wrestling — black

Writing — brown

Yachting — red

Yoga — orange (black) + blue

APPENDIX 3. ALPHABETICAL LIST OF DISEASES AND SYMPTOMS

Acute respiratory disease (often) — green, blue, violet

Adenoids — violet

Agalmatophilia — green

Agoraphobia — black

Alcoholism — red

Allergies — orange, violet

Anorexia — orange (+ yellow)

Antritis — violet

Asthma, bronchial — violet + orange

Attention deficit disorder (in children) — red + blue

Belching — yellow, blue

Blindness — green

Bowel polyps — brown

Bronchial asthma — violet + orange

Bulimia — yellow

Claustrophobia — red

Compulsive gambling — red

Conjunctivitis — green

Constipation — brown

Coughing — yellow

Crohn's disease — brown

Cystitis — red

Deafness — blue

Déjà vu — green

Dental caries — yellow

Depression — blue, violet, blue + red

Diarrhea — brown

Drug addiction — red

Dry mouth — yellow

Duodenal ulcer — blue

Dysbiosis — brown

Enuresis — red

Epilepsy — brown, (black)

Erotomania — red

Esophagitis — yellow

Exhibitionism — green

Falling (often) — black

Fear — green, violet

Frigidity — green, blue, violet

Fungous disease — orange

Gastritis — blue

Gerontophilia — red

Glomerulonephritis — red

Gluttony — yellow

Gonorrhea — red

Gout — red

Hallucinations, audio — blue

Hallucinations, visual — green

Head cold — violet

Hemorrhoids — brown

Hyperactivity — red

Hyperthermia — red

Hypertonia — red, black, orange

Hypothermia — green, blue, violet

Hypotonia — blue, green, violet

Hysteria — green

Immunodeficiency (congenital) — green, blue, violet

Impotence — green, blue (red)

Irritable bowel syndrome — brown

Itching — orange

Kleptomania — orange

Masochism — orange

Muteness — yellow

Narcissism — green

Nasal polyps — violet

Necrophilia — black

Nephrolithiasis — red

Neurodermatitis — orange

Nymphomania — red

Oral herpes — yellow

Otitis — blue

Paranoia — violet

Phobias — green, violet

Pimples — orange

Promiscuity — red

Psoriasis — orange

Pyelonephritis — red

Pyromania — red

Rhinitis — violet

Sadism — brown

Satyriasis — red

Schizophrenia — green, blue, violet, (brown)

Self-harm — black

Shortsightedness — green

Sinusitis — violet

Somnambulism — green

Stammering — yellow, brown

Stomach ulcer — blue

Stomatitis — yellow

Syphilis — red

Tearfulness — green

Temperature (always slightly high) — red

Temperature (always slightly low) — blue, green, violet

Tonsillitis — yellow

Trauma (often) — black

Urethritis — red

Vaginitis — red

Vampirism — yellow

Vegetative-vascular dystonia — green, blue, violet

Virtual reality — red + blue

Visions — green

Vitiligo — orange

Voyeurism — green

Zoophilia — black